Easy Research Paper

You Can Do It!

By Ceil Humphreys

Easy Research Paper

Written and Illustrated by Ceil Humphreys

http://prhe.net/resources/easy-research-paper/

ISBN-13: 978-0-9852897-2-0

Published by Tanglewood Publishing

Printed in the USA.

Tanglewood Publishing
Fortress Book Service
1607 Tanglewood Dr.
Clinton, MS 39056
601-924-5020

www.tanglewoodpublishing.org

Picture of author courtesy of Breter Photography

Cover by Indi Images

Layout by Martha Nichols/aMuse Productions

FORTRESS
BOOK | SERVICE

BEST OF THE BEST IN EVERY ACADEMIC DISCIPLINE

Many thanks to my husband Wesley,

who supports me in everything I do,

to all my teaching colleagues

who have shared their wisdom over the years,

to my students,

who have always been a source of encouragement and joy in my life,

and to my son Rob,

who gave his time and expertise to edit this book for me.

TABLE OF CONTENTS

Introduction vii

PART I THE BASICS—
ONE BITE AT A TIME 1

   BITE ONE   Select a Topic........................ 3
   BITE TWO   Gather information 5
   BITE THREE   Bibliography Cards 13
   BITE FOUR   Taking Notes 17
   BITE FIVE   The Outline......................... 25
   BITE SIX   Writing the Rough Draft 31
      Bibliography........................... 37
      Footnotes............................. 37
   THE LAST BITE   The Finished Product 41

PART II EXTRA INFORMATION FOR THOSE
WHO WANT TO GO THE
EXTRA MILE 43

Writing Hints   45
Tools For Teachers................................... 55
   Suggested Schedule 55
   Teacher Helps   59
   Bibliographic Grading Rubric......................... 61

Sample Outlines and Grading Rubrics	
Beginning—Animal...........................	62–65
Intermediate—State in the USA...............	66–76
Intermediate—Country......................	77–91
Advanced—Person from History..............	92–105

Why I Wrote This Book............................. 109
About the Author 111

INTRODUCTION

So, you have to write a research paper, and you don't know where to start.

Never fear; you can do it!

There's a saying:

How do we eat the elephant?

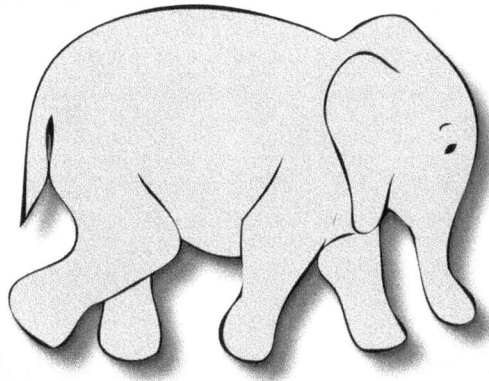

One bite at a time.

Your paper is a great big elephant that I am going to help you eat, one easy bite at a time.

Before you know it, you'll be all done and the proud author of a fantastic research paper.

So let's get started.

PART I

THE BASICS—

ONE BITE AT A TIME

BITE ONE

SELECT A TOPIC

Maybe your teacher has told you what to write about, or you may be able to choose your own topic. Here are some guidelines.

Make it interesting!

- Pick something that interests you. You are going to be spending a lot of time on this topic, and it really helps if you find it interesting.

- Make sure your topic isn't so broad that there's no way you can cover it all.

- If you can come up with a question to answer, that is also helpful, especially for a scientific paper.

- Be sure you will be able to find enough information to write about. An obscure person from history may be very interesting, but the amount of information on that person may be limited. Choose someone who will be easier to learn about.

BITE TWO
GATHER INFORMATION

Time to visit the library. Yes, the library, that place with all the books where you have to be very quiet because people are studying.

In the old days, people had sets of encyclopedias in their houses, and their children used those books to write their reports. But the teachers said a good report must come from many sources, not just an encyclopedia, so off they went to the local or school library.

Multiple, varied sources = a good paper

Fast forward to today: People have computers in their houses, and their children get information from the Internet and write reports using the material from websites. But the teachers still say that a good report must come from many sources, not just the Internet. Besides, some of those sites are not reliable. So, off we go to the good old library again.

There are wonderful, informative books and resources at the library that people don't have at home. Spend some time at the library actually holding some of those books in your hands. You may not need them for this report, but it's good to know they are there, and you may need them in the future. The librarians are paid to help you, so tell them what you're doing and ask for their help. It's your tax money at work.

Following are several pages I have my students take to the library when they start their reports. It gives them a little tour of the library and acquaints them with the resources that are available. Technology is changing every day, and your library may store information in a different way than what's listed here. The main thing is to know what's available so you can access it when you need to. Besides, you may meet someone interesting while you're there. They also have videos and CDs you can check out for free, so have some fun, too.

The library can actually be a fun place to go if you know where to look.

LET'S TAKE A TOUR OF THE LIBRARY

Have you ever noticed all those numbers on the end of the book-shelves or on the spine of a book? It's a system developed by Melvil Dewey (1851–1931) back in the old days as a way to classify and organize books so they will be easy to find. It is based on the number 10, therefore the name....

THE DEWEY DECIMAL SYSTEM

The ten major classes are

000-099   General Works (Biography, Computers, Information)

100-199   Philosophy, Psychology, Ethics

200-299   Religion and Mythology

300-399   Social Sciences (Sociology, Education, Government)

400-499   Languages

500-599   Sciences and Mathematics

600-699   Technology (Engineering, Medicine, Cooking, Gardening)

700-799   Fine Arts (Art, Music, Drama, Recreation)

800-899   Literature

900-999   History, Geography, Travel

Each class can be divided into 10 smaller classes, and each of those into 10 more classes, and so on. It's like the key to a map.

THE CARD CATALOG

Back in the day, if you wanted to find a book in the library, you went to a big, wooden cabinet with lots of drawers that contained cards on each book. These days we use computers to search for books. This is the information you can find:

- Call number (Mr. Dewey's special number for that book)
- Author
- Title
- Edition
- Number of pages
- Subject headings
- Copyright date

GET CARDED

If you don't have a library card, get one today. You will also need it to access the library website later.

SEEK AND YE SHALL FIND

Do a book search at the library by the subject you are researching and see how many books or magazine articles you can find. Print a copy of the report and use it to help you find books and materials on your subject. Some may be at a different location, and your librarian can have them sent to you.

HINT: Check out the juvenile section first, even if you're all grown up.

Later, you can also access the library from home, and you'll need your library card—so hang on to that card!

> **BIG HINT:** You may not be able to find an entire book on your subject. That's OK. A book with only a paragraph or two is just as good (sometimes better) if it gives you the information you need.

> **ANOTHER BIG HINT:** I like to search the juvenile section first. Books for adolescents have a great way of distilling the information into the most important facts and giving a broad overview, which is very helpful at first. Later you can fill in with more detailed information.

WHY CAN'T I JUST USE THE INTERNET?

Trust me, we will later. But right now, we're going to start our search for information at the library. Besides, there may be an ice cream store nearby.

YOU CAN'T TAKE IT WITH YOU

REFERENCE BOOKS

Go on a scavenger hunt at the library and find some treasure!

There are many other helpful books you can use, but they are not allowed be checked out and taken home. They are called *REFERENCE* books and are in a special section of the library.

You will want to take lots of coins to make copies of the pages of these books. While you're at it, be sure to get all the information you need for your bibliography.

Find the reference section and the following books to get this information:

- **World Almanac** (current year)
  Pick a state and find the name of its governor. Notice all the other information you can find in this book.

- **Biographical Dictionary**
  Pick a famous person and find his or her date of birth. What other information is listed?

- **World Atlas**
  Pick a country and find it on a map. Find major cities from that country and any rivers or mountain ranges.

What other information is available?

- *Bartlett's Familiar Quotations*

  Pick a famous person and find a quotation from (or about) him or her. This is actually a fun book to read if you have the time.

- And, yes, those famous **ENCYCLOPEDIAS**!

  Find your topic in an encyclopedia at the library and copy that page (or pages). Write down the bibliographical information you need for that source.

- **VIDEOS**
  Check the VIDEO selection to see if there are any about your topic. If they are not in the library at that time, you can usually ask to have them mailed to your house.

Go ahead and get some fun videos for when you're relaxing after a hard day at the library. You deserve it!

You have just finished bite two of the elephant!

WHAT NOW?

So, you are all loaded up with books, encyclopedia articles, and maybe even a few videos about your subject. What do you do now? Go shopping, of course!

Time to go shopping!

On your way home, stop off at the office supply store and buy index cards. You'll need one package of 4 x 6 cards and several packages of 3 x 5 cards. This is really important. Buy a fancy pen or pencil you like a lot that will make it fun to do all that writing.

A highlighter will be helpful, too.

While you're at it, go ahead and get a binder for your report when it's all done. I like the kind with a clear front, three prongs to hold the papers inside, and a cardboard or plastic back.

Then take a break and get something good to eat to build up your energy level. Watch those fun videos you checked out, and relax. You've done enough for today.

PLANNING YOUR SCHEDULE

IT FEELS SO GOOD!

procrastination = bad
getting ahead = good

Always try to stay a little ahead of schedule.

If you plan ahead and get started right away, you can set your own little deadlines and avoid that last-minute panic most of us experience the day before a big paper is due.

Probably the hardest part of writing a paper is having the self-discipline to actually make yourself get the job done.

Let's play some games with our heads and force ourselves to spread out the work so we can get it done and also have time left over for fun.

Here's a schedule for how much time to allow yourself to complete each part of the paper. By now you've already chosen your topic and gathered books and materials, so we'll start from here.

SCHEDULE

- Taking notes: This is the longest part; give yourself at least half of the time left.

- Organizing the outline: Do this as you're taking notes, and that will give you more time later.

- Writing the rough draft: About a quarter of the time left (at least a week)

- Revising and editing; making final copy: This part takes only a few days.

SAMPLE ONE-MONTH SCHEDULE

- Weeks 1 and 2: Take notes. Try to be more than halfway done by the first week.

- Week 3: Organize your outline. (You can combine this with note-taking.)

- Week 4: Write the rough draft; revise and edit, make final copy.

BIG HINT: Always try to be ahead of your schedule. You never know when the flu will hit or someone offers you tickets to a game or concert that you really want to attend. Besides, it feels really good to be ahead of schedule, so go for that good feeling. Procrastination may be fun for the moment, but no one enjoys that gnawing feeling in your stomach when you still have work to do. Psych yourself out and be ahead of your own schedule. You'll be so glad you did.

Create a calendar to help you plan your time. Set aside a few days to relax, too.

Sunday	Monday	Tuesday	Wednesday	Thursday	Friday	Saturday

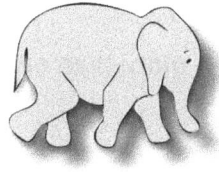

BITE THREE

BIBLIOGRAPHY CARDS

[*Biblio* = Book *(Gk.)* + *Graph* = To write or draw *(Gk.)*]

Most papers require a *bibliography* or *works cited* page.

This is a list of every resource you used to get information for your paper.

If you write down this information now, before you take the first note, you will be *very* happy later on, I promise. (See page 34 for proof.)

Use the larger **4 x 6 cards** for your bibliography.

Later you will use the **3 x 5 cards** for taking notes.

BOOKS

- Name of author, last name first

- Title of book (underlined)

- City where published (if more than one city, choose the one closest to you)

- Name of publisher

- Copyright date

- Number each source

Forbes, Esther   1

Paul Revere and the World He Lived In

Cambridge, Massachusetts

The Riverside Press

ENCYCLOPEDIAS

- Author of article (if given)

- Title of article (in quotation marks)

- Name of encyclopedia (underlined)

- Copyright date of encyclopedia

- Number of the volume (usually a roman numeral)

- The pages you used

- Number each source

```
    (no author)                              6

    "Silversmithing"

    World Book Encyclopedia


    2010
```

INTERNET SOURCES

Yes, we will use the Internet, but only as a last resort.

- Name of author, last name first (if given)

- Title of article (if given)

- Title of the website

- Document date (if given)

- Internet address

- Date you logged on (day month year)

- Number the source (This is my third source.)

```
    Smith, John                              3

    "General Robert E. Lee"

    American Civil War

    1997

    www.americancivilwar.com

    (15 April 2000)
```

This is how it will look in your bibliography:

Smith, John. "General Robert E. Lee." *American Civil War.* 1997
    www.americancivilwar.com (Retrieved 15 April 2000).

For other sources, such as magazines or videos, or for more
information on the bibliography, see page 34.

NUMBER IT

Assign a number to each resource. Example: *World Book
Encyclopedia,* source #2. Later, when you take notes from that
source, you will put its number on each note card. Some teachers
require that every fact be footnoted. Numbering each resource will
help tremendously.

LABEL IT

It's always a good idea to put your name on everything in case you
leave it somewhere. I suggest printing a bunch of labels and
sticking them to each card, or at least label the container that you
keep everything in. A plastic bag with a zipper closing works great.

STORE IT

As you find and use additional sources, always remember to make a
bibliography card first thing and keep the cards somewhere safe
where they won't get lost. This will make your life SO much easier
when it's time to write the bibliography. You sure don't want to be
running back to the library trying to find all of this information
later down the road. Do it now and be happy later.

BITE FOUR

TAKING NOTES

(This is a big bite, so get ready.)

Back to the old days. We wrote pages and pages of information in a spiral notebook, then when the time came to write, we sat and stared at the paper and didn't have a clue where to start.

Don't let that happen to you.

Follow my advice, and I promise that writing your paper will be a snap.

First, we are going to ditch the spiral notebook and replace it with lots and lots of 3 x 5 ruled index cards. I'll tell you why later.

Each card will have **ONE** fact on it. That's all. *One fact.*

One fact or idea per card.
That's all.
One.

And no complete sentences, either, unless it's a direct quote that you are going to footnote. That will save you from accidentally plagiarizing someone else's work, which is a huge no-no.

Why are we using cards? Because when the time comes to organize your notes, you will be able to arrange those cards in the order you

17

want to present your information. You will literally make stacks of cards that should go together into one paragraph.

For instance, if you are writing about a person, you may have one stack for his early life, one for his accomplishments, and one for his later life. If you have two or more facts on one card that go in separate stacks, that's no good; you would have to tear the card in half. One fact per card.

Later, you will take each stack of related facts and arrange them in the order they should be presented; for example, put the early life information into chronological order. Can you see how that will make writing the outline a piece of cake? Organization is the key, and it all starts right now in the note-taking step.

So here we go.

HOW TO COMPLETE A NOTE CARD

- Every fact you use must be documented.
- It should be on a 3x5, ruled index card and contain the following information:
- Heading from outline (ex: early life or accomplishments)
- One fact only
- No complete sentences unless it is a direct quote that will be footnoted
- Each card should be numbered by the source (top right).
- This will correspond to the number on the bibliography card from your source.
- Numbering each note card will also be helpful when it's time to make footnotes.

Below is a sample note card about Meriwether Lewis. It is from my fifth source.

Early life	**5**
asked by Pres. Thomas Jefferson	
to be his personal secretary –1801	

Here is a note card about the state of Virginia. It is from source #7.

General info	**7**
Motto: *Sic Semper Tyrannis*	
Latin for "Thus Always to Tyrants"	

NOTE-TAKING PRACTICE

If you're not familiar with taking notes, this little exercise will help you. Read the following paragraph about horses and complete the note card below it. See next page for answers that would be appropriate for a beginner's level.

What to feed your horse:

Hay or grass is essential to every horse. Horses need hay; they cannot live without it. There are different types of hay. Call local feed stores to find out what types they sell. Also, letting a horse graze from pasture is good too, but you have to make sure that the pasture is safe and there are no poisonous plants your horse could eat.

Every horse needs water. Horses drink between 6 and 9 gallons of water a day. Water should be kept clean, and it should be changed often. It should be clear, and it shouldn't smell bad. The horse should be able to drink whenever it wants to, and the water should not be really cold or really hot. Frozen or icy water will discourage the horse from drinking, and it may drink very little, or get sick. Horses don't like hot water, either. Dirty, frozen, or smelly water can also cause colic.

Oats are a good source of energy. Oats contain fats, starches, and a good percentage of protein (11%).

Corn lacks protein, but is high in energy and fat. It is somewhat indigestible, but it can be mixed with other grain.

Barley boiled is good to put condition on a horse.

from source #6 The Ultimate Horse Site ultimatehorsesite. com/info/feeding.html

I have underlined the basic information below. This is appropriate for a beginner's level.

What to feed your horse:

<u>Hay</u> or <u>grass</u> is essential to every horse. Horses need hay; they cannot live without it. There are different types of hay. Call local feed stores to find out what types they sell. Also, letting a horse graze from pasture is good too, but you have to make sure that the pasture is safe and there are no poisonous plants your horse could eat.

Every horse needs <u>water</u>. Horses drink between 6 and 9 gallons of water a day. Water should be kept <u>clean</u>, and it should be changed often. It should be clear, and it shouldn't smell bad. The horse should be able to drink whenever it wants to, and the water should <u>not be really cold or really hot</u>. Frozen or icy water will discourage the horse from drinking, and it may drink very little, or get sick. Horses don't like hot water, either. Dirty, frozen, or smelly water can also cause colic.

<u>Oats</u> are a good source of energy. Oats contain fats, starches, and a good percentage of protein (11%).

<u>Corn</u> lacks protein, but is high in energy and fat. It is somewhat indigestible, but it can be mixed with other grain.

<u>Barley</u> boiled is good to put condition on a horse.

from The Ultimate Horse Site http://www.ultimatehorsesite. com/info/feeding.html

This is from source #6, The Ultimate Horse website

6

Habitat and behavior

eats hay, grass, oats, corn, barley

drinks clean water, not too hot or cold

CH

Card size is 3 x 5"

Heading from the outline

One idea only

No complete sentences

My initials identify the card as mine.

"HOLEY" RESEARCH, BATMAN!

Maybe your teacher gave you an outline to follow, but chances are you will have to come up with one of your own. No problem, you can do it.

I have known students to write the paper, then write the outline, because an outline was required. That's like shopping at the grocery store, then coming home and making a list.

The purpose of the outline is to help you organize your information. You may think it's a pain, but if you do it, writing the paper will be easy as pie. Well, almost. It will be a lot easier than if you don't write an outline, I guarantee you.

Five minutes of planning is worth fifteen minutes of looking.
—Claudia

If you ever read *From the Mixed-Up Files of Mrs. Basil E. Frankweiler* by E. L. Konigsburg (and I highly recommend it), Claudia and her little brother Jamie were given one hour to find the clue to a mystery they were trying to solve. Jamie wanted to jump right in and start searching Mrs. Frankweiler's files, but Claudia said to wait; five minutes of planning were worth 15 minutes of looking. You'll have to read the book to see what happened, but I'll tell you this: Claudia was right.

Long before you finish taking notes, start an outline. Begin organizing your information, and see what direction you want your paper to take.

Once a former student of mine was writing a college paper about Auschwitz, and he was stuck. He had lots of information but didn't know how to organize it or where to begin. I advised him to start with a brief history of Germany around the time of World War I, the terms of the treaty after the war, the Great Depression and how it affected the Germans, rise of German nationalism and Hitler, and World War II. That would put Auschwitz into the context of the time and explain how it came to be instead of just jumping into information about the concentration camp.

He took my advice and made an A on his paper. I was so proud, but I told him that next time he wanted my help, it had to be about a happier subject!

The outline is the blueprint for your paper. As you take notes, start to form an outline and insert information into it on a regular basis. This will help you see what facts you've already got and decide what direction your paper will take. It will also show you what I call "holes" in your research—areas where you still need to find more information.

Continue to take notes and fill in your outline. The more details, the better. I've never heard of a teacher counting off for too many details.

Lots of details = good research

If you work on your outline as you go along, you will find yourself ahead of the game when the time comes to create the outline. At this point you can take a little breather or go straight into the rough draft and *really* be ahead!

But first some rules....

BITE FIVE

THE OUTLINE

If you have to turn in your outline for a grade, then you want to do it right. Outlines have very strict rules for capitalization and punctuation. Read these carefully.

RULES FOR PROPER OUTLINE FORM

I. First main idea
   A. Subheading—supports first main idea (I)
      1. Detail—supports subheading A
      2. Detail—supports subheading A
         a. Detail—supports subheading 2
         b. Detail—supports subheading 2
            i. Detail—supports subheading b
           ii. Detail—supports subheading b
   B. Subheading—supports first main idea (I)
II. Second main idea
   A. Subheading—supports second main idea (II)
   B. Subheading—supports second main idea (II)
      1. Detail—supports subheading B
      2. Detail—supports subheading B

RULES FOR EVERYTHING ELSE ON THE OUTLINE

1. Roman numerals are used for main points.

2. Capital letters are used for subheadings.

3. Arabic numerals are used for supporting details.

4. Lowercase roman numerals are used for details under Arabic numerals.

5. A period is placed after each number and letter in the outline.

6. Every point in the outline begins with a capital letter.

7. Other words start with a lowercase letter unless a proper noun or pronoun.

8. There are no periods after any of the points in the outline.

9. Each level of the outline is indented and lined up under like headings.

10. If there is an A, there is also a B. If there is a 1, there is also a 2.

11. Each point is stated as a topic, not as a complete sentence.

GOOD FORM

Use parallel form, meaning, state things the same way.

KINDS OF AMERICAN COLONIES

Not Parallel	*Parallel*
I. Colonies that are in the north	I. Northern colonies
II. Some colonies were in the middle	II. Middle colonies
II. Colonies to the south	III. Southern colonies

PRACTICE YOUR NEW KNOWLEDGE

Correct the following excerpt from an outline about George Washington.

I. Early life

A. Place and Date of Birth

    1. Westmoreland County, Virginia

    2. he was born on Feb. 22, 1732.

    3. he grew up on Ferry Farm.

B Parents

1. father

    a Augustine Washington was his father

    b Virginia planter—tobacco

    c modestly wealthy

    2. mother—Mary

3. Lawrence was his half brother.

    a. George inherited Mount Vernon from Lawrence.

    b. George lived with Lawrence as teenager.

See next page for answers.

Answers to correct outline about George Washington.

CORRECTED OUTLINE

I. Early life

A. Place and **d**ate of **b**irth   **Capitalize first word only unless proper noun.**

    1. Westmoreland County, Virginia

    2. Feb. 22, 1732   **No complete sentences, no periods at the end.**

    3. Ferry Farm   **No complete sentences, no periods at the end.**

B. Parents

    1. **F**ather   **Capitalize first word of each entry.**

        a. Augustine Washington   **No complete sentences**

        b. Virginia planter—tobacco   **Put a period after each letter or numeral of the entry.**

        c. **M**odestly wealthy   **Capitalize first word of each entry. Put a period after each letter or numeral of the entry.**

    2. **M**other—Mary   **Capitalize first word of each entry.**

    3. Half-brother Lawrence   **No complete sentences, no periods at the end.**

        a. Left Mount Vernon to George   **Indent each new entry. No complete sentences, no periods at the end.**

        b. George lived with as teenager   **Indent each new entry. No complete sentences, no periods at the end.**

HELP!

OK, this is a lot to learn, especially if no one has ever taught it to you. At the end of this document, I have included four sample outlines, including "holes" in the research.

Beginner (elementary to middle school level):
    Outline about an ANIMAL   page 62
Intermediate (middle to high school level):
    Outline about a STATE in the USA   page 66
    Outline about a COUNTRY   page 77
Advanced (high school to college level):
    Outline about a famous PERSON   page 92

I have provided these to serve as a model of what an outline should look like and also the kind of information it should contain.

I hope you will see that once you have a well organized, detailed outline, all that's left is making it into sentences. You are *way* over the hump by now and rounding the bases to home plate. (How's that for mixing metaphors?)

Over the hump! Rounding the bases to home plate!

It's time for a big pat on the back. You are almost done; Bite Five is devoured, and it's time for the next step....

BITE SIX

WRITING THE ROUGH DRAFT

Think of the outline as the skeleton of your paper.

Now you're going to add the muscles and flesh it out.

The hardest part is behind you; you're skating downhill from here.

Ideally, you have every single fact in your outline that's going into your paper. At this point, that's all you need in front of you. Give yourself about a week to do this part; don't rush it. Of course, this time period is going to vary according to the length of your paper and how much time you have left before it's due.

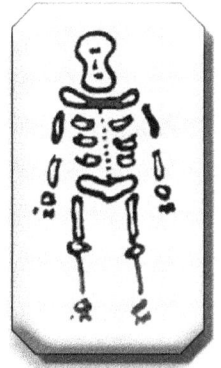

Day 1
Divide your outline into about four parts. Every day, using your outline, start writing one part (usually a roman numeral or two). You can write by hand if you want to, but I recommend a word processor instead. Don't worry about making it fabulous or anything, just make sentences. We'll fix it up later. When you're all done with that day's section, put it away and don't think about it anymore that day. As Alton Brown says on *Good Eats* when he's mixing up quick bread, "Just walk away."

Day 2

Look at what you wrote yesterday. It's probably awful. That's OK, because now you are going to revise and edit it. Go through the Revise and Edit Checklist on the next page and make corrections. Then start on the next section and make it into sentences. Put it down when you're finished, and go have some fun.

Day 3

Revise and edit Day 1 again and Day 2. Make your changes. Write the next section. Walk away. Go have fun.

Day 4

Are you starting to see a pattern here? Revise and edit what you've written, write some more, walk away, go have some fun. You're all done with the writing part; all you have to do now is revise and edit some more. The elephant is almost all gone.

Day 5

Revise and edit one more time. Get a friend or two or a former teacher who is a good writer/editor to look it over and make suggestions. It's good to plan this in advance, as it takes some time to do it right. Buy that person a nice gift, by the way, because editing a paper takes a lot of time and is a lot of work. Go back and make all corrections, then go out and celebrate.

All that's left of that elephant is about one tiny bite!

REVISING AND EDITING CHECKLIST

All sentences

__ are complete.

__ begin with a capital letter.

__ tell specific facts.

__ end with correct punctuation.

Paragraphs

__ Each paragraph starts with a topic sentence.

__ Topic sentence contains general, introductory information, not specific details.

__ Each paragraph is about one main idea.

__ Sentences in each paragraph tell about its main idea.

Writing

__ Sentences are combined to be more interesting.

__ Exact, specific words are used. Be concise.

__ Details are included about each item on the outline.

__ All words are spelled correctly.

__ No errors in grammar, punctuation, or word usage.

For more writing hints, see page 45.

BACK TO THE BIBLIOGRAPHY

Chances are you will have to include a bibliography with your paper. No problem; you already have the information. All you have to do is type it in the correct format.

"The time to be happy is now."
—My friend Dina's favorite quote

This is the part where I said, "Do it now, be happy later."

Your teacher may have a preference for which format he or she wants the bibliography (or works cited) page to follow. One example is the MLA (Modern Language Association) format. You can find directions on the Internet or at a college bookstore. Be sure to follow those directions very carefully. Capitalization, punctuation, italics, and indenting must be precise and according to the format.

The following are the instructions my students use.

HOW TO COMPLETE A BIBLIOGRAPHY

Your *bibliography* (*biblio* = book; *graph* = to write or draw) is a written list of all the books and other sources used in researching your paper. It should be on a separate piece of paper after the body of your report. Sometimes the bibliography is called *"works cited."*

Here are the rules for writing your bibliography. **Be sure to follow them exactly.**

FOR A BOOK

- Alphabetize the entries by the last name of the author, comma, first name, then a period.

  Humphreys, Ceil.

- For two or more authors, follow the same procedure as with one author, put a comma, then write the other authors' names in regular order (first name then last name), with the word *"and"* before the last author, followed by a period.

  Humphreys, Ceil, Bill Clifton, Will Colclasure, Gwen Gurr, and Haley McAfee.

- Type a period after the author's name and then type one space.

- Write the title of the book. If handwriting, underline it. If typing, it should be in italics.

- Type a period followed by one space.

  Humphreys, Ceil. *My Life and Times.*

- Type the city in which the book was published (if more than one city is listed, use the one closest to you), followed by a colon and one space. Type the name of the publishing company, followed by a comma, a space, and the date of publication, followed by a period.

  Humphreys, Ceil. *My Life and Times.* Orlando: Acme
      Publishing, 2002.

- Begin each entry at the left margin line. If the entry is longer than one line, indent the remaining lines of the entry. This is called *reverse* or *hanging indent.* Do NOT write on the next line until you have used the entire space all the way to the right margin line. Skip one line between entries.

  Humphreys, Ceil, Bill Clifton, Will Colclasure, Gwen Gurr, and
      Haley McAfee. *How to Teach Homeschoolers in a Way that Is
      Both Fun and Academically Challenging.* New York:
      Homeschool Press, 2003.

FOR NEWSPAPER OR MAGAZINE ARTICLES

- For authors of articles, use the same guidelines as for listing authors of books, and type one space.

- After the author's name, write the title of the article in quotation marks. Type a period inside the end quotation mark and type one space. Next, type the title of the magazine or book in which the article appeared. Type it in italics or underline it if writing by hand. Type a comma and one space. Type the date of publication, a colon, a space, and the page number of the article, followed by a period.

  Clifton, Bill. "Finding the Thumbprint of
      the Creator in All of Nature." *Creation
      News Monthly*, Sept. 2002: 99-100.

Bibliography		
Name, date, class number	5	
3-5 sources	5	
Alphabetical order	5	
Reverse indented	5	
Punctuation rules followed	5	
Capitalization rules followed	5	
Proper form for entries	10	
Turned in on time	10	
Total	**50**	

REMEMBER

✓ ABC order by author's last name.
✓ Reverse indent all entries.
✓ Follow all punctuation rules.
✓ Be sure to spell and capitalize correctly.

HINT: To reverse indent, type your entire entry, allowing the text to wrap to the next line naturally. When you are all done, click at the end of the first line and hit ENTER. Then click at the beginning of the second line and hit TAB. Do the same for any remaining lines. On the next page is a sample bibliography that shows how to cite many different kinds of sources.

HERE IS A GUIDE TO THE TYPE OF SOURCE EACH ENTRY ON THE NEXT PAGE REPRESENTS

Clifton—magazine article

Combee—text book

Greek—encyclopedia, no author listed

Harmon—Internet website

Humphreys, Ceil—book

Humphreys, et al.—book with multiple authors

Humphreys, Rob—newspaper article

Netzorg—reference book with author

Whale—CD software for computer

Writing—TV production (prod. stands for producer)

BIBLIOGRAPHY

Clifton, Bill. "Finding the Thumbprint of the Creator in All of Nature." *Creation News Monthly*, Sept. 2002: 99-100.

Combee, Jeffrey. *History of the World in Christian Perspective*. Pensacola: A Beka, 1979.

"Greek Temples." *Encyclopedia Hellena*. 2000 ed., 293-295.

Harmon, Mark. "Early Italian Renaissance Innovator Giotto." *The Artchive*. http://artchive.com/artchive/G/giotto.html (Retrieved 11 Feb. 2003).

Humphreys, Ceil. *My Life and Times*. Orlando: Acme Publishing, 2002.

Humphreys, Ceil, Bill Clifton, Will Colclasure, Gwen Gurr, and Haley McAfee. *How to Teach Homeschoolers in a Way that Is Both Fun and Academically Challenging*. New York: Homeschool Press, 2003.

Humphreys, Rob. "How I Became a Newspaper Editor." *Culpeper Star-Exponent* 19 Mar. 2001: B2.

Netzorg, Rebecca. "Making Valentines for Fun and Profit." *Creative Crafts Encyclopedia*. 2002 ed.

Whale, Shamu. "How to Swim Fast." *Underwater News*. 2000-2001 ed. CD-ROM. Atlanta: Software for Kids, Inc. 1998.

Writing a Research Paper. Prod. Wesley Humphreys. PRHE Special. WABC, Orlando, 12 Jan. 2002.

FOOTNOTES

Your teacher may require you to include footnotes. That means that when you quote a source directly, you give credit to the source in a little note at the bottom of that page. Some people use endnotes instead, which are like footnotes, but the information is at the end of the paper instead of at the bottom of each page.

Let's say you are quoting Pliny the Younger when he gave an eye-witness account of the eruption of Mount Vesuvius in A.D. 79. In your paper you quote your source directly:

> Pliny the Younger described the eruption of Mount Vesuvius as "a cloud of unusual size and appearance…its general appearance can best be described as being like an umbrella pine, for it rose to a great height on a sort of trunk and then split

off into branches, I imagine because it was thrust upwards by the first blast and then left unsupported as the pressure subsided, or else it was borne down by its own weight so that it spread out and gradually dispersed."[1]

At the bottom of that page, you will tell where that quote came from. The footnote for the Pliny quote is at the bottom of this page.

When mentioning a work for the first time, include all information for that source.

(indent) Author's name, *Title of Book* (City where published: Publisher, copyright date), page.

> **HINT:** How to make the little number at the end of the sentence:
>> At the end of your quote, type the number of the footnote. Then highlight that number and click on the x^2 tab on the toolbar or choose the superscript function.

Do the same thing when you type the footnote information at the bottom of the page.

What on earth is an ibid.?

Sometimes in books you will see ibid. or op. cit. Ibid. is from the Latin *ibidem*, meaning "in the same place." Op. cit. is from the Latin *opere citato*, "in the work cited." These terms aren't used much anymore, but it's good to know what they mean.

In footnotes or endnotes citations, the term Ibid. means that you are quoting the same book two times in a row.

[2] Ibid. 17-18.

These days, the author's last name and the page number are used instead.

[2] Carey 17-18.

Footnote in place.

---

[1] John Carey, *Eyewitness to History* (New York: Avon Books, 1987) p. 16.

There are many types of sources that may need to be footnoted, and your teacher may prefer a certain method.

Otherwise, a good resource is *MLA Handbook for Writers of Research Papers* by Joseph Gibaldi. Or you can also find many examples on the Internet.

Here's how this source would look in your bibliography:

Carey, John, Ed. *Eyewitness to History.* New York: Avon Books, 1987.

Here's how this source would look as a footnote:

1   John Carey, *Eyewitness to History* (New York: Avon Books, 1987) p. 16.

Notice that the bibliography indention is different for a bibliography entry than it is for a footnote.

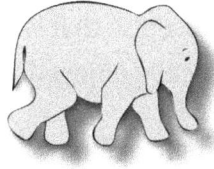

THE LAST BITE

THE FINISHED PRODUCT

YOUR MASTERPIECE

In your hands you hold your *magnum opus*, your great work. Are you going to slam it with a stapler and throw it on the teacher's desk? No way! You are going to make it beautiful. Impress that teacher from the get go with your great work ethic and attention to detail, and finish it off right.

Make a cover page with the title of your paper and a nice illustration of your topic. Type your name, the date, and class information at the bottom.

Punch it all with a three-hole punch and attach it in a report folder with a clear front. These can be found at office supply stores. Do your teacher a favor and don't use one of those slide-lock things. Your teacher will not be amused picking up your scattered papers off the floor when they slide out of that folder. Also, no one wants to carry home a stack of gigantic three-ring binders to grade, so make it slim.

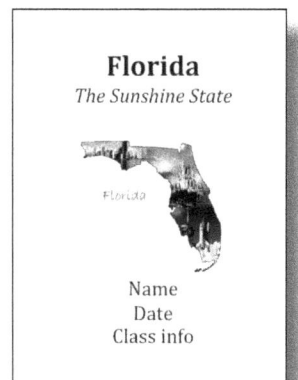

Florida
The Sunshine State

Name
Date
Class info

Some stores that specialize in copying can even bind it for you.

Attach your bibliography, outline, and anything else your teacher requires in the folder, too. It doesn't hurt to add a few photos, graphs, illustrations, or anything else that shows you did more than you had to and that you really enjoyed your topic.

Some teachers give extra credit for papers turned in early. See if you can score some extra points and also impress your teacher by being done early.

Then, when all of your friends are sweating it out and producing a sloppy, hurriedly composed, stress-filled paper at the last minute, you are relaxing and enjoying your favorite pastime.

RIP, research-paper elephant! May you rest in peace.

Happy writing!

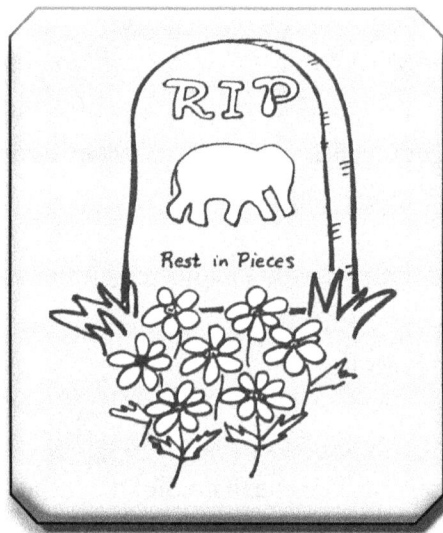

R.I.P., research paper elephant!

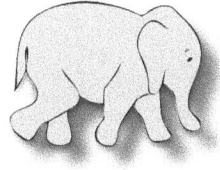

PART II

EXTRA INFORMATION

FOR THOSE WHO WANT TO

GO THE EXTRA MILE

WRITING HINTS

STRUCTURE OF A GOOD PAPER

Whether you are writing a single paragraph or a doctoral thesis, papers need to be organized.

A SINGLE PARAGRAPH

A paragraph starts with a **topic sentence** of general information that introduces that subject. This is also called the *thesis statement*. You don't just start right in with facts. You tell us right off what you're writing about or what your position is on a certain issue.

> My dog is so talented.

Next is the *body of the paragraph* where you prove the statement you just made. Load it with facts to convince us your thesis statement is true.

> Rover cannot only sit up, shake hands, and stay, he can also turn light switches on and off, shop in the grocery store, and pull a wheelchair.

After you have given lots and lots of details, it's time to conclude (if it's a single-paragraph essay) or transition to the next paragraph.

> I am so proud of my Canine Companion. (Concluding a single paragraph)

> My cat, on the other hand, lives only for herself. (Transitions to the next paragraph, which is about the cat)

MAKE A SANDWICH

My friend Patti Lash used to bring all the ingredients for a sandwich to her fifth-grade classroom to show her students how to write a good paragraph. She would hold up two pieces of bread and tell how they are like the topic sentence and concluding sentences that hold the paragraph together.

Next, she'd add meat between the bread, to represent the facts and details.

Lettuce, onion, tomato, pickles, mayonnaise, and other condiments that make the sandwich really tasty represented descriptive words, action verbs, similes, metaphors, and other literary devices that spice up our writing and make it enjoyable to the reader.

When her students entered my classroom the next year in the sixth grade, boy oh boy, could they write! They always remembered that sandwich, and so do I, many years later.

Make your writing like a delicious, mouth-watering sandwich, held together by a topic sentence and concluding sentence and filled with details and descriptions inside. Yum!

MULTIPLE-PARAGRAPH ESSAYS

The format is the same for a longer essay, but now instead of one topic sentence, we use an **introductory paragraph**.

It contains the **thesis statement** and other general information that serves as a preview of what is in the rest of the paper.

This is usually written after the outline has been composed.

Each paragraph that follows must start with a **topic sentence**.

Don't just jump in with details. Then follow with lots of detail sentences that support the topic sentence. Finish with a **transition sentence** that leads you into the next paragraph.

Just like that sandwich needed a piece of bread on the bottom, your paper needs a **conclusion.** It mirrors the introduction and wraps up the paper. This is not the time to introduce new material, but instead to remind the reader of what you've been saying.

Don't just leave your paper hanging; bring it to a close.

MORE ON THE STRUCTURE

INTRODUCTORY PARAGRAPH—should contain very general information only, no specific details. Its purpose is to introduce the paper and set the tone. The thesis statement is an integral part of the introduction. The introductory paragraph is to a research paper what a topic sentence is to a paragraph.

CONCLUSION—a mirror image (but not the exact same words) of the introductory paragraph. It wraps up the paper and restates the introduction, plus it may reach some conclusions. It also does not contain specific details. It and the introductory paragraph are like the bookends of the paper; they hold it together.

NO, NO, NO:
> My report is about …
> The purpose of this paper is to…
> I hope you enjoyed my paper about …
> So now you know all about ….

YES, YES, YES:

(Intro) George Washington, the father of our country, was a true hero.

(Conclusion) Without the strong Christian and moral leadership of George Washington, the United States may never have become the great nation it is today.

All paragraphs must have a topic sentence that introduces the material that will be presented in that paragraph. It is a general statement and should not include any details.

NO: Charles "the Hammer" Martel drove the Moors out of France in 732.

YES: France has endured a long history of defending herself against intruders.

Paragraphs should end with either a concluding sentence or a sentence that makes a transition to the next paragraph.

HOW TO MAKE YOUR WRITING STAND ABOVE THE REST

The best source for good writing is *The Elements of Style* by William Strunk, Jr. and E. B. White. Everyone should own a copy. This little book is worth its weight in gold. By the way, that's E. B. White who wrote *Charlotte's Web*, so you know it's good.

The following is very general information that I have compiled after years of editing and grading research papers. Look over these hints carefully, and use them when revising and editing your paper.

DON'T GET PERSONAL

In a **formal** paper, all pronouns are in the third person (he, she, it, they), never first person (I, we) or second (you). It is acceptable to use "one" when referring to a person, but it sounds very stiff and formal.

Keep your personal opinion out of a formal paper. Never mention yourself. You can state a fact (George Washington was the first president) but not an opinion (I think George Washington was a great man).

Pretend you're writing for an encyclopedia article. In an **informal** paper or narrative, you can use second—or third-person pronouns and/or mention yourself. Your language can also be less formal.

MAKE IT COMPLETE AND VARYING

- All sentences must be complete sentences.

- Vary your sentence structure to make your paper interesting.

- Check to see if many sentences are starting the same way. If so, change the beginning.

  Florida has a warm climate. It is very hot. It has many beaches. It is a place where tourists like to come. It has Disney World.

  It, it, it... *Boring*! Every sentence starts the same way.

- Also, combine several short sentences into a longer, more interesting one.

  NO: George Washington wanted to go to sea. His mother wouldn't let him. He became a surveyor instead.

  YES: Because his mother wouldn't allow him to become a sailor, George Washington became a surveyor instead.

- Every paragraph should be indented about four to five spaces.

- Do not leave an extra line between paragraphs.

- Keep all verbs in past tense when writing a historical paper.

  George Washington was the leader of the Continental Army.

- It is acceptable for verbs to be in present tense when writing about things that are in the present.

  Elizabeth II is the Queen of England.

Here are some general tips that will make your writing stand above the rest.

- Write out numbers one through ten. Use numerals for 11 and up. If a sentence begins with a number, always spell it out.

  Ninety-three percent of the people over age 25 can read.

- NEVER use ampersands (&) or etc. in a paper.

- Compass directions are not capitalized unless they are proper nouns.

  Take a right and go north on Northeast Avenue.

- Use the correct term. Think when you write.

it's = it is	BUT	*its* = belonging to it
you're = you are	BUT	*your* = belonging to you
they're = they are	*there* = a place	*their* = belonging to them

- A formal paper is *formal*. Don't say "here," meaning the United States. Say "children," not "kids." Use superlatives sparingly.

  The amazingly spectacular scenery is enjoyed by kids here, too!

  No! no! no! (By the way, no exclamation points, either!!!)

- When referring to people, use "who" or "whom." When referring to things, use "that."

  The person **who** sits next to me gave me a granola bar **that** she brought.

- When typing, type one space after a comma or semicolon and one space after the end of a sentence.

- "A lot" is two words, not one, but it doesn't sound very good in a formal paper.

- When using ordinal numbers, use *first, second, third*, not *firstly, secondly, thirdly*.

- *Lastly* is not a word, by the way. Use *finally* instead.

- When writing, pretend that you have to pay $1 for every word you use. Get your message across using the fewest words possible. That's called being concise.

  NO:
  The dog that belongs to Tom

  YES:
  Tom's dog (You just saved yourself $4!)

- Use a person's entire name the first time you mention him or her. After that, use the last name only.

  George Washington was born in Virginia. … Washington fought in the French and Indian War.

- Use spell check for misspelled words. Have a friend look it over, too.

- Watch your capitalization, especially on proper nouns like names, rivers, countries, cities, battles, holidays, and languages.

- Commas and periods *always* go inside quotation marks.

- Write out words instead of abbreviating.

  World War I, not WWI.

LET'S GET REALLY PICKY

- **Since** has to do with time.

  Since I left high school, many things in my town have changed.

- **Because** has to do with cause and effect.

  Because he practices hard every day, he can shoot three-pointers.

- A country or state is a single noun and is referred to by *it*, not *their*.

  Mexico has a president as leader of its government.

- *People* is a plural noun and is referred to by **their**. See the difference?

  The people of Mexico have a president as the leader of **their** government.

- When you discuss the gross national product, it is not capitalized, but initials (GNP) are.

- Compass directions are not capitalized, but areas of the country are (the wild, wild West; the old South). When referring to Europe and America as the *Western* world, capitalize it.

- **Between** involves two people; **among** indicates three or more.

- Things you can count are **fewer.** Amounts are **less.**

  Eat *less* catsup and *fewer* french fries.

A SHORT PUNCTUATION REVIEW

- All sentences must end in a period, question mark, or exclamation point. (Exclamation points are not appropriate in a formal paper and should be used mostly for dialogue, in my opinion.)

- If you shove two complete sentences together, there are three ways to punctuate.

    1. If there's a conjunction (joining word like and, or, but), use a comma.

        I like ice cream, **and** chocolate is my favorite flavor.

    2. If there's no joining word, use a semicolon. The two ideas need to be related.

        I like ice cream; chocolate is my favorite flavor.

    3. Or just make two separate sentences and use a period.

        I like ice cream. Chocolate is my favorite flavor.

- Colons (:) are used for a list after the word "following."

    I like the following flavors of ice cream: chocolate, vanilla, and strawberry.

- You do not use a colon when giving a list without the word "following."

    The ice cream store has chocolate, vanilla, and strawberry flavors.

HOW TO PUNCTUATE DIALOGUE

"Oh, Ashley, Ashley," sighed Scarlett as she gazed into his handsome face and fanned herself with her handkerchief.

*   "Frankly, my dear," said Rhett, "I don't know what you see in the fellow. How about me instead?"*

"You?"

"Yes," he replied, "me."

Meanwhile, Ashley was telling Melanie that he loved her.

- Always indent when a new person speaks, even if it is only one word.

- Capitalize the first word the person says unless the sentence is interrupted.

- Use commas and quotation marks to set off the person's actual words. If it's a paraphrase, then no quotation marks are needed.

Here are samples of excellent writing from some of my former students.

INTRODUCTORY PARAGRAPH

With its ancient history and modern industries, beautiful coastal towns and scenic islands, majestic mountains and active volcanoes, Italy is a country filled with wonder from its top to its toe. Recognizable from space, the boot-shaped country has molded both ancient and modern world history. Its fashion, marble, and automobile industries set today's standard throughout the world. Italy is known for its history, heritage, people, cuisine, fashions, mountains, beaches, and climate.   (Elena Chong)

Australia is an island, a country, and a continent all in one, with deserts, rain forests, and snow-capped mountains that make it an interesting place to explore. Many plants and animals found in Australia are unique and are found nowhere else in the world. Australia has many attractions, making it a real wonderland.

(Joshua Sheppard)

Switzerland is a small European country known throughout the world for its magnificent scenery, especially its snow-capped mountains. It is a land full of adventurous, artistic, and individual people. Switzerland is not just a land of yodeling, watch-making, skiing, and to-die-for chocolate, it is one of the world's oldest democracies. The Swiss people love their country and are proud of their long tradition of freedom.   (Jared Winn)

TOPIC SENTENCE

Rough and untamed describes much of Afghanistan's geography.   (Elena Manubens)

The tale of Israel begins with Abraham, Isaac's father.   (Brooke Alvarado)

The people of the Netherlands are proud of their rich and exciting heritage.   (Miranda Lytle)

CONCLUSION

Togo is "Little Africa." With varied climates, geography, and cultures, Togo provides the variety found all over Africa. A blend of the old and new, closely held tribal beliefs and customs have made room for change and modern technology to strengthen this small but influential nation.   (Ellen Smith)

TOOLS FOR TEACHERS

Students may use these as examples to follow, and teachers may find them useful, too.

Following are sample outlines and grading rubrics for papers on three levels:

- Beginning level (elementary to middle school)
  Paper about an ANIMAL

- Intermediate level (middle to high school)
  Paper about a STATE or COUNTRY

- Advanced level (high school and beyond)
  Paper about a PERSON

Any of these papers could be used at any level.

The structure is the same, but more details would be expected at higher levels.

SUGGESTED SCHEDULE

I teach homeschool children, and they come to class only one day a week, so everything is on a weekly schedule. Here is the timeline I use for the research paper.

Before Christmas Holidays—Choose Topic

No more thinking about it until Christmas is over.

After Christmas

Take a field trip to the library and complete Library Research Skills paper. Check out books and other resources.

Complete bibliography cards on those books.

They don't start note-taking yet until I teach that skill.

First Week Back from the Holidays

I conduct a workshop for the moms so they will know what I am teaching the children. This takes almost two hours, and I go over everything I will cover in the next two or three months.

I teach the students how to complete a note card.

Next Three Weeks

They take notes. I do periodic note card and bibliography card checks to make sure no one is lagging behind.

Week 3

I teach how to complete an outline and have them start filling out their outlines as they finish their research, looking for "holes" in their research.

Week 5

Outlines are due. They are not allowed to start writing until I have checked and approved their outlines.

I teach how to complete a bibliography, and they type their bibliographies at home this week while I am checking outlines.

If the outlines are not complete or up to standard, I return them, and the students keep working. I usually do this by e-mail.

Checking the outlines and doing it right is very labor intensive.

Week 6

I teach how to write the paper, and they start on their rough drafts. This takes two weeks to complete.

They turn in their bibliographies, and I grade them this week.

Week 8

Rough drafts are due. For most people, this would be the actual finished product, but my goal is for them to have a perfect paper (or as close as we can get), so I call this the rough draft. I edit the papers and return them the following week. This is so much easier when they have followed directions, but any way you look at it, it's a brutal week for the teacher. Don't make any social engagements this week!

In class I teach about how to write a speech, and we watch the video *Learn Public Speaking* by the Standard Deviants.

> www.StandardDeviants.com *or* 800-238-9699
> ISBN 1-58198-478-2

They write their speeches this week; I grade their rough drafts.

Week 9

I return the rough drafts, and they start making all the corrections at home, plus they assemble everything needed for the final report.

They turn in typed copies of their speeches and also work on their presentations.

Week 10

Final copies due. BIG celebration!

I have a "golden treasure box" that a student's mom gave me several years ago, and the papers go into that. I take photos of the students holding their papers and wearing their "I worked hard, and I am so proud of myself" faces.

We draw numbers to see who will give speeches on which dates, then they wheel and deal with each other to get the date they want.

By now it's spring break, and we all need a good rest.

Next 3–4 Weeks

Each student gives a three- to five-minute speech about his or her topic, which includes the most interesting and important information about the topic. It is NOT a reading of the complete paper.

Parents, grandparents, siblings, neighbors, everyone is invited to come. I schedule five to six students per afternoon session.

They can make posters, dress up, bring artifacts to share, or make a PowerPoint presentation. The more creativity, the better.

Each presenter also brings a snack to share that goes with the topic. For example: food that a country or state is known for. This gets really interesting when the topic is a person. We have eaten Michelangelo brand lasagna, pizza that looked like King Henry VIII, and even headless cookies that represented his wives. One student who researched Stonewall Jackson brought lemonade, because Jackson loved it, and another made a chocolate chip cookie shaped like the state of Georgia and lit birthday candles that were stuck with frosting into the vicinity of Atlanta. As a Georgia girl, it was so hard for me to give him an A+ on his paper about General Sherman, but he earned it.

Through it all, my job is not just teacher, but also coach and encourager. I want them to experience the satisfaction of working really, really hard on something, sticking with it, and how very good it feels to be all done and know you've done your best.

TEACHER HELPS

On the following pages are sample outlines and grading rubrics that I use. I like to teach by modeling, so I provide the outline for the students to follow. By high school, they should be able to create their own outlines.

Feel free to use these teacher helps or modify them to meet your needs.

ALL LEVELS	Bibliography grading rubric
BEGINNER LEVEL	Animal
INTERMEDIATE LEVEL	State, country
ADVANCED LEVEL	Historical person

Name_____ Date ___ / ___ / ___ Class # ____

Attach this page to the front of your bibliography.

FOR A BOOK

1. Alphabetize the entries by the last name of the author, comma, first name, then a period. For two or more authors, follow same procedure as with one author, put a comma, then write the other authors' names in regular order (first name then last name), with the word "*and*" before the last author, followed by a period.

2. Type a period after the author's name and then type one space.

3. Write the title of the book. If handwriting, underline it. If typing, it should be in italics. Type a period followed by one space.

4. Write the city in which the book was published, followed by a colon and one space. Then write the name of the publishing company, followed by a comma, a space, and the date of publication, followed by a period.

5. REVERSE (HANGING) INDENT: Begin each entry at the left margin line. If the entry is longer than one line, indent the remaining lines of the entry. Do NOT write or type on the next line until you have used the entire space all the way to the right margin line. Skip a line between entries.

FOR NEWSPAPER OR MAGAZINE ARTICLES

1. Follow the same guidelines for listing authors of articles that you would for books.

2. Following the author's name, write the title of the article in quotation marks. Place a period *inside* the closing quotation marks. Type one space. Then write and then underline or type in italics the title of the magazine or book from which the article comes.

3. Insert one space after the publication's title. Give the date of publication, followed by a colon, a space, and the page number of the article. End with a period.

Other: See guidelines in the bibliography section of this book.

Bibliography		
Name, date, class number	5	
3–5 sources	5	
Alphabetical order	5	
Reverse indented	5	
Punctuation rules followed	5	
Capitalization rules followed	5	
Proper form for entries	10	
Turned in on time	10	
TOTAL	50	

Beginning Level Paper on an ANIMAL
Outline Guidelines

Introductory paragraph with thesis statement.

I. General information
    A. What is its Latin name? (extra: Kingdom, Phylum, Class, Order, Family, Genus, Species)
    B. Is it domesticated or wild?
    C. Is it a mammal, fish, bird, or reptile?
    D. What is a group of them called? (example: a pride of lions)
    E. Are there other members of this family? (example: horse family—zebras, donkeys)

II. Appearance
    A. How large does it get? (length, height, and weight)
    B. Does it have scales, fur, or what on the outside?
    C. How many and what kind of legs, fins, wings, or other body parts? (extra credit: drawing of animal with parts labeled)
    D. What colors or other special markings?
    E. What are the male and female names? (example: male—stallion, female—mare)

III. Habitat and behavior
    A. Where does it live? (continents, also type of area like mountains or desert)
    B. What does it eat?
    C. Does it travel in a herd or is it solitary?
    E. How does it communicate with other animals? (example: whinny)
    F. Do other animals try to eat it? Which ones? (use words *predator* and *prey*)
    G. How does it defend itself? (example: run away, climb a tree, bite with sharp teeth)

IV. Offspring
    A. How long is the female pregnant?
    B. Does she give live birth or lay eggs?
    C. How many babies does she usually have at a time?
    D. What are the babies called?
    E. Can the babies see/walk/take care of themselves when they're born?

   F. How do the parents watch over the young ones?
   G. What is its average life expectancy?
V. Uses and importance
   A.   Is it used for food by people? If so, who and how?
   B. Does it do work for people? (example: pull a plow, riding for sports like polo, racing)
   C. Is its hide, fur, or scales used to make things? (hooves— glue; hide—leather)
   D. Are there any famous ones? (example: Clydesdales)

Conclusion: Wrap up your paper with a short paragraph of general information that mirrors the introduction.

This shows what your outline will look like.

Horses

Thesis statement: It's hard to imagine the world without horses. They are fun to ride, and they have also been very useful to man throughout history.

I. General information
   A. Latin name
      1. *Equus caballus* (domestic horse)
      2. *Equus ferus caballus* (wild horse)
   B. Mostly domesticated
   C. Mammal
   D. Herd
   E. Other members
      1. Zebras
      2. Donkeys
II. Appearance
   Continue to fill in information.

NOTE: Latin names of animals (and plants) are typed in italics.

Conclusion: From holding generals during battles and pulling plows, to helping disabled children, the horse has played an important part in the history of the world.

Here's what that first paragraph (after the introduction) could look like.

> The horse is a very interesting animal. Most horses, or *Equus caballus*, are domesticated for man's use. However, a few wild horses, or *Equus ferus caballus*, still live on their own, not on ranches or with people. The horse is a mammal, and in the wild, it lives in a group called a *herd*. Other members of the horse family include zebras and donkeys.

Grading Rubric for Outline on an ANIMAL	pts
Introduction (general info, no specific details)	10
I. General information Latin name (EC: Kingdom, Phylum, Class, Order, Family, Genus, Species) Domesticated or wild; Mammal, fish, bird, or reptile; Group called; other members of family	15
II. Appearance Size (length, height, and weight); scales, fur; Body parts; colors or markings; male/female names	15
III. Habitat and behavior Where live; what eat; travel in a herd or solitary; Communicate; other animals eat it (predator and prey); Defend itself	15
IV. Offspring How long female pregnant; live birth or eggs; How many babies; babies called; Babies see/walk when born; parents watch young; Life expectancy	15
V. Uses and importance Used for food; do work; hide used; famous ones	10
Conclusion (general info, wrap up paper)	5

Revision and proofreading checklist
All sentences
  are complete.
  begin with a capital letter.
  tell specific facts.
  end with correct punctuation.
Paragraphs:
  Each paragrph is about one main idea.
  Sentences in each paragraph tell about its main idea.
Writing
  Sentences were combined to be more interesting
  Exact words were used.
  Enough details were included.
	15

Other	
TOTAL	**100**

Name _____ Date ___/___/___ Class # _____

Attach this page to the back of your final copy.

1. Use 8.5 x 11 inch white typing paper.

2. Type your paper on the computer using a plain-type font such as Times or Arial, size 12. Or write it in your best handwriting, using a black pen and lined paper.

3. Double-space your paper; use the front of the paper only. Indent every new paragraph about four spaces. Do not put an extra line between paragraphs.

4. Prepare your bibliography as shown on the worksheets you were given.

5. Prepare a title page that includes

    ___ The name of your animal

    ___ A picture or drawing of your animal

    ___ Your name

    ___ The date

    ___ Your class number

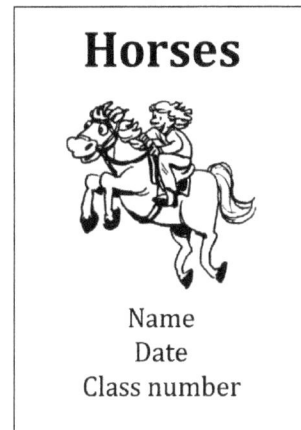

Horses

Name
Date
Class number

6. Assemble the pages in this order:

    Title page

    Body of report

    Bibliography

    Maps, charts, or pictures not already included in the body of the paper

    Outline

    Corrected rough draft

7. Attach all pages in a clear plastic binder with three brads to fasten the paper, not a slide lock.

Intermediate Level Paper on a STATE Outline Guidelines

Thesis statement and introductory paragraph.
General information that introduces your subject.

I. General information
    A. Nickname
    B. Origin of state name
    C. Motto
    D. Flower
    E. Bird
    F. Tree
    G. Song
II. Location and size
    A. In relation to U.S.
    B. Latitude and longitude
    C. Bordering states
    D. Bordering bodies of water
    E. Size
        1. Square miles
        2. Rank by state
        3. Miles long and wide
III. Climate, geography, and industry
    A. Climate
        1. Type (humid subtropical, Mediterranean, desert, etc.)
        2. Average temperatures (high and low)
        3. Highest recorded temperature and date
        4. Lowest recorded temperature and date
        5. Average annual precipitation
        6. Dangerous weather or other natural catastrophes
    B. Physical features
        1. Important geographical features (rivers, lakes, mountains, etc.)
        2. Highest and lowest points
    C. Major crops, natural resources, and industries
IV. History and important events (Be sure to tell when it became a state.)
    A. Early history
        1. Original inhabitants
        2. Explorers or conquerors
        3. First permanent settlement

  B. 1700s and 1800s (Tell involvement during major wars and other important events.)
   1. 1700s
   2. 1800s
  C. 1900s and present day (See Florida outline for more details.)
IV. People and government
  A. Governor and party affiliation
  B. U.S. senators and party affiliation
  C. Number of electoral votes
  D. Population according to the latest census
  E. Major cities
  F. Major colleges and universities
  G. Famous people (historically and current)
V. Reasons to visit the state (List and describe specific sites people visit, tourist attractions, etc.)

Conclusion: Wrap up your paper with a short paragraph of general information that mirrors the introduction.

Here's an outline I created about the state of Florida.

"The Sunshine State"

Because of its year-round warm climate and sunny beaches, Florida is a popular state, not only for tourists, but also for people moving from other states to escape harsh winters and high taxes. "The Sunshine State" boasts an array of attractions ranging from theme parks to space rockets. There is something for everyone in this beautiful state.

I. General information
- A. Nickname
    1. "The Sunshine State"
    2. Sunshine almost every day
    3. Encourages tourism
- B. Origin of state name
    1. Pascua Florida—"Flowery Easter"
    2. Named by Ponce de Leon
    3. Easter Sunday 1513
- C. Motto—"In God We Trust"
- D. Flower—orange blossom
- E. Bird—mocking bird
- F. Tree—sabal palmetto palm
- G. Song
    1. "Old Folks at Home" (Suwannee River)
    2. By Stephen Foster

II. Location and size
- A. Southeastern United States
- B. Latitude and longitude
    1. Latitude 24° 30' N to 31° N
    2. Longitude 79° 48' W to 87° 38' W
- C. Bordering states
    1. Georgia—north
    2. Alabama—northwest
- D. Bordering bodies of water
    1. Peninsula—surrounded by water on three sides
    2. Atlantic Ocean to the east
    3. Gulf of Mexico to the west
    4. Straits of Florida to the south

    E. Size
- 1. 65,758 square miles
- 2. Ranked 22nd largest state geographically
- 3. 500 miles long
- 4. 160 miles wide

III. Climate and geography

    A. Climate
- 1. Humid subtropical
- 2. Average temperatures
  - a. High 91.7° F
  - b. Low 39.9° F
- 3. Highest recorded temperature
  - a. 109° F
  - b. June 29, 1931
  - c. Monticello
- 4. Lowest recorded temperature
  - a. –2° F
  - b. Feb, 13, 1899
  - c. Tallahassee
- 5. Precipitation
  - a. Average 54 inches per year
  - b. Second only to Louisiana (55 in.)
- 6. Dangerous weather
  - a. Hurricanes and tropical storms
  - b. Tornadoes

    B. Physical features
- 1. Main rivers
  - a. St. John's River
  - b. Kissimmee River
- 2. Lake Okeechobee—largest lake within a state
- 3. Three main bays
  - a. Tampa Bay
  - b. Apalachee Bay
  - c. Florida Bay
- 4. Everglades—"Sea of Grass"
- 5. Straits of Florida
- 6. Florida Keys
- 7. Highest point
  - a. Britton Hill
  - b. 345 feet above sea level
- 8. Lowest point—sea level

C. Major crops, resources, and industries
1. Citrus
2. *(I need to do more research here.)*
3.

IV. History and important events
A. Early history
1. First inhabitants—Indians
a. Timucua
b. Apalachee
c. Calusa
d. Seminoles—from Georgia
2. First explorer
a. Ponce de Leon—1513
b. Looking for "Fountain of Youth"
c. Claimed for Spain
3. First permanent settlement
a. St. Augustine
b. 1565
c. Spanish
d. Burned in 1586 by Sir Francis Drake (English)

B. 1700s and 1800s
1. 1700s Florida under Spain
a. 1763 ceded to Great Britain by Spain
b. 1783 returned to Spain
c. 1819 sold to USA
d. 1821 became U.S. territory
2. 1800s
a. Seminole War
b. 1835–42
c. Andrew Jackson
d. Most Native Americans sent to Oklahoma
3. Entered Union
a. March 3, 1845
b. 27th state
4. Civil War
a. 1861 seceded from Union
b. Joined Confederacy
c. 1868 readmitted to Union
5. Spanish-American War
a. 1898
b. Cuba seeking independence from Spain

This is a lot of information. Younger students may not need to include this much.

    c. Tampa launching point of U.S. troops

    d. Teddy Roosevelt and Rough Riders

C. 1900s and present day

    1. World War I

       a. Produced food for war

       b. Many naval bases in FL

    2. 1920s

       a. Land boom—developers

       b. More cars and vacationers

       c. Land bust 1926

       d. Great Depression 1929

    3. Citrus industry—1929

       a. Mediterranean fruit fly

       b. Citrus production cut 60%

    4. World War II

       a. Training area for soldiers

       b. Transportation system updated

    5. Post-war population growth

       a. Cuba

       b. Haiti

    6. Walt Disney World opens 1971

       a. Increased tourism

       b. More jobs

    7. Population from other states

       a. Favorable climate

       b. No state income tax

       c. Jobs

    8. Present day

       a. Good interstate highway system

       b. Many international airports

       c. Large university system

       d. High-tech industries

       e. U.S. space program

       f. Tourism strong

V. People and government

  A. Governor—Rick Scott (R)

  B. U.S. senators

    1. Marco Rubio (R)

    2. Bill Nelson (D)

  C. Electoral votes—25

  D. Population—15,982,378 (2000)

It's easy to get bogged down in the history section. Just hit the high points, but be sure to give information about each decade or era, especially during wars and other major historical events.

Bring it all the way to the present.

    E. Major cities
1. Capital—Tallahassee
2. Jacksonville—mouth of St. John's River
3. Miami—famous for South Beach
4. Tampa—large Cuban population
5. Orlando—many tourist attractions
    F. Famous people
1. Osceola—Seminole Indian leader
2. Pat Boone—singer
3. Dwight Gooden—baseball player
4. Marjorie Kinnan Rawlings—author
5. Burt Reynolds—actor
6. Clarence Thomas—Supreme Court judge
VI. Reasons to visit the state
    A. Beaches
    B. Everglades National Park
    C. St. Augustine—oldest permanent city in U.S.
    D. Kennedy Space Center
    E. Florida Keys
    F. Attractions
1. Walt Disney World—Orlando
2. Universal Studios—Orlando
3. Sea World—Orlando
4. Busch Gardens—Tampa
5. Legoland—Winter Haven
6. Silver Springs—Ocala

Conclusion:

With an array of natural attractions such as its beaches and warm climate, to the man-made attractions like theme parks and the space center, Florida is a great state to visit. It is also a great place to live, as many people have discovered, causing its population to continue to increase, in spite of the threat of hurricanes. "The Sunshine State" is indeed a bright spot on the map of the United States.

Name _____ Date ___/___/___ Class # _____

Grading Rubric for Outline about a STATE	pts
Name, date, class number, guidelines page attached	5
Introduction (general info, no specific details)	5

I. General information
    A. Nickname   E. Bird
    B. Origin of state name   F. Tree
    C. Motto   G. Song
    D. Flower   10

II. Location and size
    A. In relation to U.S.   D. Bordering bodies of water
    B. Latitude and longitude   Square miles; rank by state;
    C. Bordering states   miles long & wide   10

III. Climate and geography
    A. Climate: Type; average temp (high and low)
        highest & lowest recorded temperature
        average annual precipitation; dangerous weather or
        other natural catastrophes
    B. Physical features
        Important geographical features
        (rivers, lakes, mountains, etc.); highest and lowest points   10

IV. History and important events (when it became a state)
    A. Early history: Original inhabitants; explorers or
        conquerors; first permanent settlement
    B. 1700s and 1800s (involvement during major wars
        and other imp events) 1700s; 1800s; 1900s and today   20

V. People and government
    A. Governor and party affiliation
    B. U.S. senators and party affiliation
    C. Number of electoral votes
    D. Population according to the latest census
    E. Major cities
    F. Famous people   10

| VII. Reasons to visit the state (List specific sites people visit.) | 10 |
| Conclusion: (general info, wrap up paper) | 5 |

All outline rules followed:
  1. Roman numerals are used for main points.
  2. Capital letters are used for subheadings.
  3. Arabic numerals are used for supporting details.
  4. A period is placed after each number and letter in the outline.
  5. Every point in the outline begins with a capital letter.
  6. There are no periods after any of the points in the outline.
  7. Each level of the outline is indented.
  8. If there is an A, there is also a B. If a 1, also a 2.
  9. Each point is stated as a topic, not as a complete sentence.
 10. Parallel form is used.   15

| TOTAL | 100 |

Name _____ Date ___/___/___ Class # ____

Attach this page to the front of your ROUGH DRAFT.
Attach your edited and corrected outlines to the back.

Grading Rubric for Rough Draft about a STATE	pts
Guidelines sheet attached	5
Introduction (thesis statement, general info, no specific details)	5
I. General information (topic sentence) Nickname; origin of state name; motto; flower; bird; tree; song	10

II. Location and size (topic sentence)
 In relation to U.S.; latitude and longitude; bordering states;
    bordering bodies of water; size; square miles; rank by state;
    miles long and wide
	10

III. Climate and geography (topic sentence)
 Climate: type; average temp (high and low); highest and
     lowest recorded temperature; average annual precipitation;
     dangerous weather or other natural catastrophes
 Physical features: important geographical features (rivers,
     lakes, mountains, etc.); highest and lowest points
	10

IV. History and important events (topic sentence)
 Early history: original inhabitants; explorers or conquerors;
    first permanent settlement (when it became a state)
 1700s and 1800s (involvement during major wars
    and other imp events) 1700s; 1800s; 1900s and today
	20

V. People and government (topic sentence)
 Governor and party affiliation; U.S. senators and party affiliation;
    number of electoral votes; population according to the 2000
    census; major cities; famous people
	10

VII. Reasons to visit the state (topic sentence) List specific sites people visit.	10
Conclusion: (topic sentence) General info, wrap up paper	5

Revision and proofreading checklist:
 All sentences
    are complete.
    begin with a capital letter.
    tell specific facts.
    end with correct punctuation.
 Paragraphs
    Each paragraph starts with a topic sentence.
    Each paragraph is about one main idea.
    Sentences in each paragraph tell about its main idea.
 Writing
    Sentences are combined to be more interesting
    Exact words are used.
    Details are included about each item on the outline.
    All words are spelled correctly.
    No errors in grammar, punctuation, or word usage
	15

TOTAL	100

Name _____ Date ___/___/___ Class # ____

Final Copy Guidelines for Paper about a STATE

1. Use 8.5 x 11 inch white typing paper.

2. Type your paper using a plain-type font such as Times or Arial, size 12.

3. Double-space your paper; use the front of the paper only.

4. Indent every new paragraph about four spaces. Do not put an extra line between paragraphs.

5. Prepare your bibliography as shown in the bibliography section.

6. Prepare a title page that includes

   ___ The name of your state

   ___ Your state's nickname

   ___ Your state's flag

   ___ Your name

   ___ Your class number

   ___ The date

7. Assemble the pages in this order:

   Title page

   Body of report

   Bibliography

   Maps, charts, or pictures not already included in the body of the paper

   Outline

   Edited (by teacher) outline

   Edited (by teacher) rough draft

   Grading rubric (see next page)

8. Attach all pages in a binder with a clear plastic front. **Use the kind that fastens with brads and not a slide lock**. These can be found at office supply stores.

Name _____ Date __ / __ / ____ Class # ____

Attach this paper in the back of your research report binder.
Attach your edited outline and rough draft.

Grading Rubric for Final Copy of STATE Research Paper	pts
Guidelines page attached	5
Content	
Thesis statement and introductory paragraph	10
Paragraph to cover each topic in guidelines	
General information	20
Location and size	20
Climate and geography	20
History: Early, 1800s, 1900s, present day	20
People and government	20
Reasons to visit the state	20
Conclusion	10
Organization	
Was the outline followed?	5
Style	
Grammar, capitalization, punctuation, spelling	10
Sentence construction	10
Presentation	
Typed, double spaced, in a report folder	10
Bibliography	10
State flag and map	10
TOTAL	200

Intermediate Level Paper on a COUNTRY Outline Guidelines

Introductory paragraph with thesis statement

I.   Location and climate
    A.   Location
        1.   Continent
        2.   Hemisphere
        3.   Latitude and longitude
    B.   Bordering areas
        1.   Countries
            a.
            b.
            c.
        2.   Bodies of water or other geographical formations (if applicable)
            a.
            b.
            c.
    C.   Size
        1.   Square miles
        2.   Equivalent to U.S. state (ex. size of the state of Georgia)
    D.   Climate
        1.   Type (humid subtropical, Mediterranean)
        2.   Temperatures
            a.   Average daily temp
            b.   High in summer
            c.   Low in winter
        3.   Average yearly amount of rainfall
    E.   Cities
        1.   Capital city
            a.   Where located
            b.   Other information about the city
            c.
        2.   Other important cities and interesting facts about them
            a.
            b.
            c.

You may need more or fewer letters in each of these categories.

II. Physical geography
   A. Famous land forms (include major rivers, mountains, deserts, etc.)
      1.
      2.
      3.
   B. Major natural resources (list in order of importance)
      1.
      2.
      3.
   C. Major crops
      1.
      2.
      3.
   D. Wildlife native to the country
      1.
      2.
      3.
III. History and heritage
   A. Original inhabitants
      1.
      2.

> *This is the largest part of your paper. You will need many more numbers in each of these categories. See the sample USA outline for more.*

   B. Brief history of major events of country in chronological order (include famous rulers, conquerors, wars, inventions, cultural events)
      1. B.C. times
      2. First five centuries
      3. A.D. 500–1000
      4. A.D. 1000–1500
      5. Last 500 years
      6. Last 50 years
IV. People and culture
   A. Number of people
   B. Population growth in percent
   C. Major ethnic groups
      1.
      2.
      3.
   D. Major religions
      1.
      2.
      3.
   E. Language(s) spoken and why

> *Most of this information can be found in a current world almanac or on your country's website.*

F. Major holidays and customs
    1.
    2.
    3.
G. Foods your country is known for
    1.
    2.
H. Education
    1. Average years of education per student
    2. Literacy rate
    3. Who goes to school
    4. Ages children attend school
I. Health care
    1. Ratio of doctors to people
    2. Quality of health care
    3. Who pays for it (if government, try to find out tax rate on income)

V. Government and economics
    A. Government
        1. Type of government
        2. Current national leader and his/her title
        3. Name of governing body
    B. Motto or nickname
    C. National symbols
    D. Economy
        1. Type of economy (capitalist, socialist, communist)
        2. Developed or developing country
        2. GDP (gross domestic product)
        3. Average income per capita
    E. Major imports and exports
        1.
        2.
        3.
    F. Main industries
        1.
        2.
        3.

Parents and teachers, this is a good time to discuss with your students the difference between a developed and developing country and also different types of economic systems.

    G. Popular tourist sites (tell where each one is and some information about it)
        1.
        2.
        3.
Conclusion

United States of America
(sample outline)

The United States of America is a vast land with every kind of climate, landform, culture, and natural resource. This "land of the free and home of the brave" continues to open its arms to people from countries all over the world.

I. Location and climate

A. Location (48 contiguous states)

1. Continent—North America

2. Northern, Western Hemisphere

3. Latitude

a. 71°23' N (Northwest Angle, Minnesota)

b. 24°33' N (Key West, Florida)

4. Longitude

a. 66° 57' W (West Quoddy Head, Maine)

b. 124° 44' W (Cape Alava, Washington)

B. Bordering areas

1. Countries

a. Canada—north

b. Mexico—south

2. Bodies of water

a. Atlantic Ocean—east

b. Pacific Ocean—west

C. Size

1. 3,794,085 square miles

2. Includes 50 states

D. Climates

1. Continental in the Northeast and Northern Midwest

2. Humid subtropical in the Southeast

3. Steppe and desert in the Western plains

4. Mediterranean on the Western coast

5. Marine on the Northwestern coast

If you have a small country, you can put the degrees of latitude and longitude only and not put the names of the northernmost, easternmost, etc. points.

Hint: To make the degree symbol, type a lowercase o, highlight it, and press the x^2 button on your font toolbar.

There may be only one or two types of climate in a small country. Consult an atlas map of world climates to get this information.

E. Temperatures

    1. Average daily

        a. Winter—

        b. Summer—

> *This is what I call a "hole" in my research. I still need to find this information.*

> *An up-to-date World Almanac is an excellent source for this information. I happened to find more information than just the average high and low temperature, so I included it.*

    2. High

        a. 134° F

        b. Death Valley, California

        c. July 10, 1913

    3. Low

        a. –80° F

        b. Prospect Creek, Alaska

        c. Jan. 23, 1971

> *Because the USA is so big, it is hard to give an average for the entire country, so I put the extremes.*

F. Average annual precipitation

    1. Hawaii—63.7 inches

    2. Louisiana—60.1in. (highest in contiguous states)

    3. Nevada—9.5 in.

    4. Kauai Island in Hawaii—460 in. average per year

    5.

G. Cities

    1. Capital—Washington, D.C.

    2. Other important cities

        a. New York—financial center

        b. Boston—historical area

        c. Dallas—technology and oil production

        d. Los Angeles—movie-making

        e. Detroit—car manufacturing

        f. Chicago—meat packing

        g. Orlando—vacation capital of the world

> *Your country may have only one or two major cities. Put what they are known for or where they're located. I could have put lots more here, but just wanted to give you an example.*

II. Physical geography

    A. Famous landforms

        1. Rocky Mountains

        2. Great Lakes

        3. Mississippi River

        4. Grand Canyon

        5. Great Plains

> *You get the idea here. Include longest rivers, highest mountains, deserts, gorges, lakes, and any other interesting landforms in your country. If you have a large country, then choose the most famous ones.*

B. Major natural resources

1. Oil

2. Coal

3. Timber

4.

C. Major crops

1. Grains

    a. Corn

    b. USA largest producer and exporter of corn

    c. Soybeans

    d. Rice

3. Cotton

4. Tobacco

5. Fruit and vegetables

6.

D. Native wildlife

    a. Turkey

    b. Grizzly bear

    c. Bald eagle

III. History and heritage

A. Original inhabitants

    a. Indians-named by Columbus

    b. "Native Americans"

    c. Many tribes

    d. Not much known

B. Colonial era

1. St. Augustine

    a. Spanish

    b. 1565

2. Jamestown

    a. English

    b. 1607

3. Plymouth

    a. Puritan pilgrims from England

    b. 1620

4. 13 English colonies by 1775

Places where I need to do more research.

Another "hole" in my research. Don't list every animal in your country, but only the ones most associated with it or the unusual ones.

If you are searching a European country or one with a longer written history, you will have much more in the first part of this history section. Not much is known about pre-Columbus America, but we'll make up for it in the latter part of the history section.

C. Independence from Great Britain
1. Declaration of Independence July 4, 1776
2. Defeated British at Yorktown 1781
3. Constitution written 1787
4. George Washington first president

D. War of 1812
1. Great Britain impressing seamen
2. Fort McHenry—"Star Spangled Banner"
3. Battle of New Orleans—Andrew Jackson

E. Westward expansion
1. Lewis and Clark 1804–1806
2. California Gold Rush 1848
3. Transcontinental Railroad 1869
4. Desire for land

F. War Between the States 1861–1865
1. North vs. South
2. States' rights
3. Slavery

G. Reconstruction

H. Industrial expansion

I. Spanish–American War 1898
1. "Remember the *Maine*"
2. Gained Philippines, Puerto Rico, and Guam

J. World War I 1914–1918
1. "The war to end all wars"
2. *Lusitania* sunk by German submarine
3. U.S. enters 1917

K. Great Depression
1. Stock market crash 1929
2. Many out of work

L. World War II (dates) 1939–1945
1. Poland invaded by Germany
2. Pearl Harbor bombed 1941
3. Normandy invasion 1944

The history section is probably the hardest. It's easy to get bogged down in one time period and totally skip over another. Hit the highlights only.

If you are older and writing on a higher level, then add more details and explanations here.

This would be a good place to tell about things invented in America during that period.

    4. May 8, 1945 VE Day

    5. Atom bomb on Hiroshima Aug. 6, 1945

M. Korean War 1950–1953

N. Vietnam War

    1. Advisers sent 1950

    2. Escalated during Johnson's presidency in 1960s

    3. Ended by President Nixon 1973

O. Civil Rights Movement 1960s

    1. Headed by Dr. Martin Luther King, Jr.

    2. Equal rights for all regardless of race or color

P. Space race

    1. First satellite

        a. *Explorer I*

        b. 1958

    2. First American in space

        a. Alan B. Shepard

        b. 1961

    3. First American in orbit

        a. John Glenn

        b. 1962

    4. First man on the moon

        a. Neil Armstrong

        b. *Apollo 11*

        c. July 20, 1969

    5. First American woman in space

        a. Sally Ride

        b. Space Shuttle *Challenger* 1983

Q. Middle East conflicts

    1. Persian Gulf War 1990–1991

        a. Operation Desert Shield

        b. Kuwait invaded by Iraq

    2. World Trade Center and Pentagon

        a. Bombed 1993 by three Islamic militants

        b. Crashed into by planes Sept. 11, 2001

    3. Recent terrorism

        a. Afghanistan and Iraq

        b. Sponsored by Osama bin Laden

IV. People and culture

    A. 290,810,000 people as of 2003

    B. Population growth 14.1%

    C. Major ethnic groups as of 2003

        1. European—234,196,000

        2. Hispanic—39,899,000

        3. African–American 37,099,000

        4. Asian—11,925,000

        5. Native American 2,787,000

    D. Major religions

        1. Christianity

        2. Judaism

        3. Islam

        4.

The percentages or totals for each of these groups and religions are not important unless you are in high school or above. Just be sure to list them in order from largest to smallest. Be sure your information is as up-to-date as possible.

    E. Languages

        1. English

            a. Official language

            b. Originally settled by Great Britain

        2. Spanish

            a. Many immigrants from South and Central America

            b. Mostly in Florida, Texas, and California

You can see I still have some work to do on this section.

    F. Major holidays and customs

        1. New Year

            a. Parties

            b. Celebrate at midnight

        2. Easter

            a. Church services

            b. Easter egg hunts

        3. Independence Day

            a. July 4

            b. Fireworks and picnics

        4. Thanksgiving

            a. Originated with Pilgrims and Indians

            b. Big meal with family

You don't have to list every holiday they celebrate, but do include the main ones and the ones particular to that country.

5. Christmas

    a. Christmas trees

    b. Send Christmas cards

    c. Give gifts

G. Foods

    1. Hamburgers and French fries

    2. Turkey at Thanksgiving

    3. Apple pie

    4. Many foods from other countries

        a. Pizza

        b. Tex–Mex

        c. Chinese

> *Here we're looking for foods native to your country.*
>
> *This is hard for USA, as we're a nation of immigrants with many different cultural foods.*

H. Education

    1. Average years of education ____

    2. Literacy rate—____ %

    3. Public schools free to anyone

    4. Grades K–12

    5. Education compulsory ages 5–16

    6. High school graduates 84.6%

    7. College graduates 27.2%

> *This is some extra information I found on the U.S. Census Bureau's website.*

I. Health care

    1. Ratio doctors: people ____ : ____

    2. Excellent health care quality

    3. Private insurance and self-pay

    4. Government programs for poor

> *If your country pays for its citizens' health care, see if you can find out what their income tax rate is. (I'll bet it's really high!)*

V. Government and economics

A. Government

    1. Democratic republic (elected representatives)

    2. President George Walker Bush

    3. Vice President Richard Cheney

    4. Senate—two from each state

    5. House of Representatives—numbered by population

    6. Supreme Court—head judiciary

> *I found this in 2003, so my information hasn't been updated.*
>
> *Get yours as close to this year as possible.*

B. Motto or nickname

    1. In God We Trust—on money

    2. Melting pot—many immigrants

    3. Land of the free and home of the brave

C. National symbols

    1. Statue of Liberty

    2. Uncle Sam

D. Economy

    1. Capitalistic

    2. Developed country

    3. GDP as of 2003—$10.988 trillion

    4. Average income per capita as of 2003—$35,721

E. Major imports and exports

    1. Imports

      a.

      b.

    2. Exports

      a.

      b.

> *When you write the rough draft, the only thing you'll have in front of you is the outline, so be sure to include EVERY detail you need here.*

F. Main industries

    1.

    2.

G. Popular tourist sites

    1. Walt Disney World

    2. National parks

    3. Beaches

    4. New York City

    5. Grand Canyon

    6. Civil War battlefields

> *Your conclusion is very important. It will wrap up your paper and bring it all to a close. Content in the conclusion should mirror the introduction and be general information, not details.*

Conclusion

> *I think you can all get the idea of what the finished outline should look like.*
>
> *Also, I hope you can see that by the time you complete your outline, writing the paper will be a breeze. It's just a matter of turning all of this into sentences.*

Name _____ Date __ / __ / ____ _Class # ____

Attach this paper in the front of your OUTLINE.

Grading Rubric for Outline about a COUNTRY	pts
Name, date, class number, this page attached	5
I. Thesis statement that introduces the topic	5

II. Location and climate		
A. Location	D. Climate	
B. Bordering areas	E. Cities	
C. Size		15

III. Physical geography	
A. Famous landforms	
B. Major natural resources	
C. Major crops	
D. Wildlife	10

IV. History and heritage	
A. Original inhabitants	
B. Conquerors	
C. Brief history: B.C./First five centuries/A.D. 500–1000	
A.D. 1000–1500/Last 500 years/Last 20 years	20

V. People and culture		
A. Number of people	F. Major holidays and customs	
B. Population growth in percent	G. Foods	
C. Major ethnic groups	H. Education	
D. Major religions	I. Health care	
E. Language		15

VI. Government and economics		
A. Government	E. Major imports and exports	
B. Motto or nickname	F. Main industries	
C. National symbols	G. Popular tourist sites	
D. Economy		15

VII. Concluding sentence (general info, no details)	5

All outline rules followed:
1. Roman numerals are used for main points.
2. Capital letters are used for subheadings.
3. Arabic numerals are used for supporting details.
4. A period is placed after each number and letter in the outline.
5. Every point in the outline begins with a capital letter.
6. There are no periods after any of the points in the outline.
7. Each level of the outline is indented.
8. If there is an A, there is also a B. If a 1, also a 2.
9. Each point is stated as a topic, not as a complete sentence.

10. Parallel form is used.	10
TOTAL	100

Name _____ Date __ / __ / ___ Class # ____

Attach this page to the front of your ROUGH DRAFT.

Grading Rubric for Rough Draft about a COUNTRY	pts
Guidelines sheet attached, typed, double spaced	5
Introduction (thesis statement, general info, no specific details)	5
I. Location and climate (including topic sentence)	10
II. Physical geography (including topic sentence)	10
III. History and heritage (including topic sentence)	10
IV. People and culture (including topic sentence)	20
V. Government and economics (including topic sentence)	10
Conclusion: (topic sentence) General info, wrap up paper	10
Organization: Was the outline followed? Attach the edited and corrected outlines.	5

Revision and proofreading checklist:
　　All sentences
　　　　are complete.
　　　　begin with a capital letter.
　　　　tell specific facts.
　　　　end with correct punctuation.
　　Paragraphs
　　　　Each paragraph starts with a topic sentence.
　　　　Each paragraph is about one main idea.
　　　　Sentences in each paragraph tell about its main idea.
　　Writing
　　　　Sentences are combined to be more interesting.
　　　　Exact words are used.
　　　　Details are included about each item on the outline.
　　　　All words are spelled correctly.
　　　　No errors in grammar, punctuation, or word usage.   15

TOTAL	100

Name _____ Date __ / __ / ____ Class # ____

Final Copy Guidelines for a Paper about a COUNTRY

1. Use 8.5 x 11 inch white typing paper.

2. Type your paper using a plain-type font such as Times or Arial, size 12.

3. Double-space your paper; use the front of the paper only.

4. Indent every new paragraph about four spaces. Do not put an extra line between paragraphs.

5. Prepare your bibliography as shown on the worksheets earlier in this packet.

6. Prepare a title page that includes

   __ The name of your country

   __ Your country's nickname (if it has one)

   __ Your country's flag (in color)

   __ Your name

   __ The date

   __ Your class number

> **The United States of America**
> "Land of the Free and Home of the Brave"
>
> Name
> Date
> Class #

7. Assemble the pages in this order:

   Title page

   Body of report

   Bibliography

   Maps, charts, or pictures not already included in the body of the paper

   Outline

   Corrected rough draft

   Guidelines page

8. Attach all pages in a clear, flat plastic binder with three brads to hold the pages together. *Please don't use the kind that has a slide lock, as they come undone too easily.*

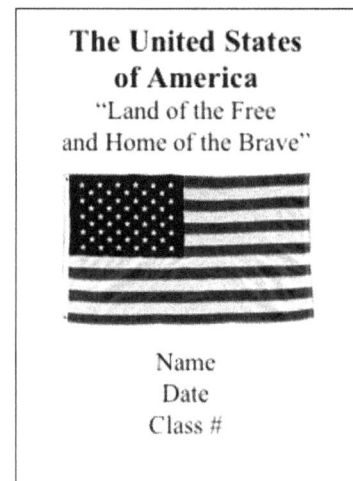

Name _____ Date __ / __ / ____ _Class # ____

Attach this paper in the back of your research report binder.

Grading Rubric for Final Copy of COUNTRY Research Paper

Guidelines page attached	5
Content	
Thesis statement and introductory paragraph	10
Paragraph to cover each topic in guidelines	
General information	20
Location and climate	20
Physical geography	20
History and heritage	20
People and culture	20
Reasons to visit the state	20
Conclusion	10
Organization	
Was the outline followed?	5
Style	
Grammar, usage, capitalization, punctuation, spelling	10
Sentence construction	10
Presentation	
Typed, double spaced, bound in a flat, clear report folder	10
Bibliography	10
Title page and country's flag	10
TOTAL	**200**

Attach your outline and edited rough draft.

Advanced Level Paper about a PERSON from History Outline Guidelines

Introductory paragraph with thesis statement

I. Early life of person
    A. Birth
        1. Place
        2. Date
        3. Anything else interesting or important you can find
    B. Family
        1. Father
        2. Mother
        3. Siblings
        4. Any other relatives or people who shaped his or her life
    C. Education
        1. Schools attended
        2. Course of study or trade learned
        3. How this prepared person or influenced his or her future
    D. Physical description
    E. Jobs held that prepared person for later life
    F. Marriage and family life can go here or in later life
II. Historical background at time person lived
    A. Political (what was happening politically during his lifetime)
    B. Religious beliefs (if they affected his life)
    C. Cultural (art, books, music, science, especially that influenced your person)
    D. Economic (state of the country at the time)
    E. Controversies (especially ones this person may have been involved in, such as slavery, women's rights, literature, art trends, etc.)
    F. Position this person took regarding the major issues of the day (if known)

> *You are setting the stage for your person and his accomplishments in this section, putting his life into the context of the age in which he lived. This is about the country or world during his time, not just about him or her. Emphasize areas in which your person was influential, such as politics, literature, music, art.*

III. Accomplishments

> *This should be the main body of your paper, two to three paragraphs.*
>
> *In chronological order, or by order of importance of the accomplishments, give the details of your person's life from young adulthood until later life.*
>
> *See the sample outline on George Washington for an example. Each major accomplishment should be a heading (capital letter) with specific details listed under each heading.*

IV. Later life of person (Some of this may be more appropriate in a different section.)
   A. Family life
      1. Spouse
      2. Children
   B. Anything not already listed under accomplishments or early life, especially concerning events later in person's life
   C. Death
      1. Cause
      2. Year and age
      3. Last words (if known)
V. Application of person's life and accomplishments to today

> *How is the world different today because he or she lived?*
>
> *This is VERY important. You will have to think long and hard about this part.*
>
> *Think of how this person impacted the world.*
>
> *This is not a recap of his accomplishments.*

Concluding paragraph

Here's a sample outline on George Washington, complete with "holes" in research.

George Washington
"Father of Our Country"

George Washington, affectionately remembered as the "Father of Our Country," was truly an incredible man. A soldier, statesman, and gentleman farmer who left his beautiful home time and again to serve his country, Washington showed his love for God in his words and actions. The United States would probably not be the great country it is today without Washington's godly leadership.

I. Early life
    A. Place and date of birth
        1. Westmoreland County, Virginia
        2. Feb. 22, 1732
        3. Grew up on Ferry Farm
    B. Parents
        1. Father—Augustine Washington
            a. Virginia Planter—tobacco
            b. Modestly wealthy
        2. Mother—Mary
        3. Half-brother—Lawrence
            a. Inherited Mount Vernon
            b. George lived with as teenager
    C. Education
        1. Mr. Hobby's "old field schoolhouse"
        2. Did not go to boarding school in England as most did
        3. Wanted to go to sea—mother objected
        4. Became a surveyor
        5. Knowledge of the land an asset during war
    D. Physical description
        1. Tall—6' 2"
        2. Reddish hair
        3. Excellent horseman
        4. "Best dancer in the colonies"
        5. *Here's a place where I need to do more research.*

II. Historical background

A. Political

1. American colonies under English rule—King George III

2. England huge imperial power

3. French and Indian War *Need the years and more background info.*

4. Anti-British sentiment in colonies

a. Taxation without representation

b. Restrictions on trade

c. Stamp Act

d. Boston Tea Party

5. Continental Congress *Explain what this was about.*

6. American War for Independence *Give lots of background info here.*

7. Federal Constitutional Convention

8. Establishment of new country

B. Religious

1. America founded on religious freedom

2. All faiths allowed

3. Colonies mostly Protestant

4. Washington—Episcopal

5. *Maybe some quotes from Washington regarding his faith*

C. Cultural

> *Washington was a political and military figure, so there should be a lot here about the country in general to set the stage for his involvement in it.*

> *This does not apply to Washington as much, so not as much information is needed as in the political realm. For a writer, composer, or artist, you will mention the major artists, etc. of the day, especially the ones who influenced or were influenced by your person and the trends in music, art, and literature.*
>
> *Mention some of the most popular dance tunes, opera, or whatever people were listening to, their composers, and the instruments they were played on. List books and authors who influenced people or were popular at that time.*

1. No aristocracy in America

2. Art *List American artists of the day, especially Gilbert Stuart*

    3. Music *List dance tunes, songs of the Revolution & British soldiers*

    4. Literature *List influential writers, especially Franklin, Paine, others*

D. Economic

    1. Strong ties to England

    2. Must sell to England only

    3. South—large plantations

       a. Tobacco and cotton

       b. Slaves

    4. Mid-Atlantic—small family farms

    5. North

       a. Industry

       b. Shipping

E. Controversies

    1. Taxation without representation *List specific acts passed by Parliament*

    2. Restricted trade

    3. American independence *Tell who was for it & who was against it.*

    4. Washington's stand *Some quotes here would be good.*

       a. Opposed taxation

       b. As farmer, disliked trade restrictions

       c. Organized resistance to British policies

       d. In favor of independence

F. Controversies while president

    1. Hamilton vs. Jefferson

       a. Backed Hamilton

          i. Funding of national debt

          ii. Assumption of state debts

          iii. Establishment of national bank

       b. Didn't favor plan for support of manufactures

    2. Other issues *Explain these in detail—tell what they were and why.*

       a. Favored American neutrality

       b. Put down Whiskey Rebellion

       c. Defeated Indians from Ohio

       d. Political parties

          i. Federalist and Democrat—Republican

          ii. Was against political parties *Quote? Why?*

III. Major accomplishments
    A. French and Indian War
        1. Age 20—adjutant in Virginia militia
        2. Colonel during war *Tell story about bullet holes through coat.*
        3. Aide to General Braddock
        4. Knowledge of the land from surveying helpful
        5. Learned how to fight like Indians
    B. Gentleman farmer
        1. Mount Vernon, Virginia
        2. Inherited from half-brother Lawrence
        3. Tobacco
    C. Continental Army—War for Independence
        1. Commander-in-Chief (2 through 10 or more, see box below)

> ***Need lots of details about battles***
> ***List all major battles, strategies,***
> ***generals, dates, results.***
>
> ***Include info about his leadership***
> ***and why he was so respected.***
>
> ***Include quotes here, too,***
> ***by and about Washington.***

        10. Defeated British—greatest military power in the world
            a. British General Cornwallis
            b. Yorktown, Virginia (Need the date here)
    D. President of USA
        1. First ever *Tell events & decisions he made during his presidency*
        2. Elected unanimously
        3. Served two terms
        4. Set many precedents *List some of the precedents here.*
        5. Refused to be king
    E. Farewell address *Give some quotes here.*
        1. September 17, 1796
        2. Rebuked party spirit
        3. Warned against "permanent alliances" with foreign powers

IV. Later life   *(Some of this could go in early life)*
    A. Family
        1. Wife
            a. Martha Dandridge
            b. Wealthy widow of Daniel Parke Custis
            c. Two children with Custis
        2. Children
            a. None of his own
            b. Adopted Martha's children
        3. Home
            a. Mount Vernon in Virginia
            b. Inherited when Lawrence died
    B. Religious beliefs
        1. Devout Christian
        2. *Quote:* _____
    C. Death
        1. December 14, 1799
        2. Cause: *Find out cause of death*
        3. "First in war, first in peace, first in the hearts of his countrymen"—*Who said this?*
V. Application of person's life
    A. Won War for Independence
    B. No longer colony of England
    C. Began a new country
    D. Set standards for presidency
        1. "So help me God" at inauguration
        2. No king for America
        3. Two terms
        4. World shocked when he stepped down
    E. Strong, devout Christian—good example of leadership

Concluding paragraph

> *Name the children and grandchildren and tell what happened to them.*

> *I'm emphasizing his Christianity, so I need some details here to prove my point, including quotes from him.*

> *Need a lot more details here of how the world is different because he lived.*

> *General information summing up your paper and reflecting the introduction*

SUGGESTED PEOPLE TO WRITE ABOUT FOR AMERICAN HISTORY

NOTE: George Washington is not on the list, because most of the examples in the research paper booklet are about him, including the sample outline.

Middle to late 1700s
Samuel Adams, John Adams, Abigail Adams, Patrick Henry, Paul Revere, Thomas Paine, Benjamin Franklin, John Jay, John Paul Jones, Thomas Jefferson, James Madison, Dolley Madison, Alexander Hamilton, Roger Sherman

Early 1800s
Meriwether Lewis, William Clark, Robert Fulton, James Monroe, Andrew Jackson, Oliver Hazard Perry, John Quincy Adams, John C. Calhoun

Mid-1800s
Daniel Webster, Henry Clay, Daniel Boone, Davy Crockett, Samuel F. B. Morse, Eli Whitney, Timothy Dwight, Sam Houston

Civil War Era
Stephen Douglass, Harriet Beecher Stowe, Harriet Tubman, Frederick Douglass, Robert E. Lee, Abraham Lincoln, Jefferson Davis, George B. McClellan, Ulysses S. Grant, Mathew Brady, Thomas J. "Stonewall" Jackson, Clara Barton, David Glasgow Farragut, William T. Sherman, James Longstreet, Joshua Chamberlain, J.E.B. Stuart

Industrial Age
Andrew Carnegie, John D. Rockefeller, Cornelius Vanderbilt, Alexander Graham Bell, Thomas Edison, Nikola Tesla, George Armstrong Custer, Chief Joseph, Dwight L. Moody, Joseph Pulitzer, William Randolph Hearst, Theodore Roosevelt, Booker T. Washington, Samuel L. Clemens (Mark Twain), Louisa May Alcott, George Washington Carver, Jane Addams, N. C. Wyeth

World War I and After

Woodrow Wilson, Gen. John Pershing, Elizabeth Cady Stanton, Susan B. Anthony, Charles A. Lindbergh, William Jennings Bryan, J. Gresham Machen, Herbert Hoover, Franklin Roosevelt, Eleanor Roosevelt, Robert Goddard, Grant Wood, Alvin York

World War II and After

Gen. George S. Patton, Gen. Douglas MacArthur, Albert Einstein, Harry S. Truman, Dwight D. Eisenhower, John F. Kennedy, Martin Luther King Jr., Georgia O'Keefe, Norman Rockwell, Jackie Robinson, Ronald Reagan

SUGGESTED PEOPLE TO WRITE ABOUT FOR WORLD HISTORY

Political/Religious Leaders

Charlemagne, Lorenzo de Medici, Niccolo Machiavelli, Pope Julius II, Pope Leo X, Oliver Cromwell, Robespierre, William Gladstone, Benjamin Disraeli, William Pitt, Winston Churchill, Charles de Gaulle, Benito Mussolini, Vladimir Lenin, Karl Marx, Joseph Stalin, Adolf Hitler, General Erwin Rommel, Chiang Kai-shek, Fidel Castro, Margaret Thatcher, David Ben-Gurion, Mahatma Gandhi, Ho Chi Minh

Explorers, Scientists and Inventors

Christopher Columbus, Francis Drake, Ferdinand Magellan, Galileo Galilei, Nicolas Copernicus, Johannes Gutenberg, Sir Isaac Newton, Charles Darwin, Johannes Kepler, Blaise Paschal, Alfred Nobel, Marie Curie, David Livingstone, Louis Pasteur

Monarchs/Conquerors

William the Conqueror, Joan of Arc, Henry VIII of England, Elizabeth I of England, Ferdinand and Isabella of Spain, Charles V (Holy Roman Emperor), James I of England, Charles I of England, William and Mary, Louis XIV of France, Louis XVI of France,

Napoleon Bonaparte, Queen Victoria of England, Wilhelm I of
Prussia & Germany, Ivan the Terrible, Peter the Great, Catherine
the Great, Czar Nicholas II

Theologians of the Reformation
John Wycliffe, Jan Hus, Martin Luther, Katie Luther (Martin's wife),
Ulrich Zwingli, William Tyndale, John Calvin, John Knox

Missionaries/ Social Reformers
J. Hudson Taylor, William Wilberforce, Florence Nightingale,
William Carey, George Muller, Amy Carmichael

Artists and Architects
Giotto, Filippo Brunelleschi, Sandro Botticelli, Leonardo da Vinci,
Albrecht Durer, Michelangelo Buonarroti, Raphael, Rembrant van
Rijn, Jacques Louis David, Pierre A. Renoir, Claude Monet, Vincent
Van Gogh, Mary Cassatt, Pablo Picasso

Writers
Desiderius Erasmus, William Shakespeare, Niccolo Machiavelli,
Dante, Charles Dickens

Musicians and Composers
Johann S. Bach, George F. Handel, Isaac Watts, Wolfgang A. Mozart
Ludwig Van Beethoven

Of course, there are many other people who have been influential
in history.

Just make sure you pick one whose information is available and
easy to find.

Name _____ Date ___ / ___ / ___ Class # _____

Attach this page to the front of your outline.

Grading Rubric for OUTLINE on a PERSON from History	pts
Name, date, class number, guidelines page attached	5
Introduction (general info, no specific details) with thesis statement	5

I. Early life of person
    A. Birth: Place, date
    B. Family: Father, mother, siblings
    C. Education: Schools attended, course of study or trade
    D. Physical description   10

II. Historical background at time person lived (Emphasize your person's place in each of these categories.)
    A. Political   D. Economic
    B. Religious beliefs   E. Controversies
    C. Cultural   10

III. Accomplishments
(The main body of your paper, 2–3 paragraphs)
    In chronological order, give details of person's life from young adulthood until later life. Each major accomplishment should be a heading (capital letter) with specific details listed under each heading.   20

IV. Later life of person
    A. Family life: Spouse, children
    B. Events not listed under accomplishments
    C. Death   Cause, year and age, last words (if known)   10

V. Application of person's life and accomplishments to today
(How is the world different today because he or she lived?)   10

Concluding paragraph	5
Quotes:: At least three direct quotes by or about your person	10

All outline rules followed:
    1. Roman numerals are used for main points.
    2. Capital letters are used for subheadings.
    3. Arabic numerals are used for supporting details.
    4. A period is placed after each number and letter in the outline.
    5. Every point in the outline begins with a capital letter.
    6. There are no periods after any of the points in the outline.
    7. Each level of the outline is indented.
    8. If there is an A, there is also a B. If a 1, also a 2.
    9. Each point is stated as a topic, not as a complete sentence.
    10. Parallel form is used.   15

TOTAL	**100**

Name_____ Date ___/___/____ Class # ____

Attach this page to the front of your rough draft.
Attach your edited and corrected outlines.

Grading Rubric for ROUGH DRAFT about a PERSON from History	pts
Name, date, class number, guidelines page attached	5
Introduction (general info, no specific details) with thesis statement	5

Early life of person (topic sentence)
    birth: place, date; family: father, mother, siblings; education:
    schools attended, course of study or trade; physical description
	10

Historical background (topic sentence)
    political; cultural; religious beliefs; economic; controversies;
    position regarding major issues of the time
	10

Accomplishments (topic sentence)
(The main body of your paper, 2–3 paragraphs)
    In chronological order, give details of person's life
    from young adulthood until later life.
	20

Later life (topic sentence)
    family life; spouse, children; events not listed
    under accomplishments; death: cause,
    year and age, last words (if known)
	10

Application of person's life and accomplishments (topic
    sentence) (How is the world different today because he
    or she lived?)
	10

Concluding paragraph (topic sentence) General info, wrap up paper	5

Footnotes
    At least three direct quotes by or about
    your person in proper footnote form
	10

Revision and proofreading checklist:
All sentences
        are complete.
        begin with a capital letter.
        tell specific facts.
        end with correct punctuation.
Paragraphs
        Each paragraph starts with a topic sentence.
        Each paragraph is about one main idea.
        Sentences in each paragraph tell about its main idea.
Writing
        Sentences are combined to be more interesting.
        Exact words are used.
        Details are included about each item on the outline.
        All words are spelled correctly.
        No errors in grammar, punctuation, or word usage.
	15

TOTAL	100

Final Copy Guidelines—PERSON from History

1. Use 8.5 x 11 inch white typing paper.

2. Type your paper using a plain-type font such as Times or Arial, size 12.

3. Double-space your paper; use the front of the paper only.

4. Indent every new paragraph about four spaces. **Do not put an extra line between paragraphs.**

5. Prepare your bibliography as shown on the worksheets you were given.

6. Prepare a title page that includes

   __ The name of the person you researched

   __ A quote about him or her or a nickname

   __ A picture of the person

   __ Your name

   __ Your class number

   __ The date

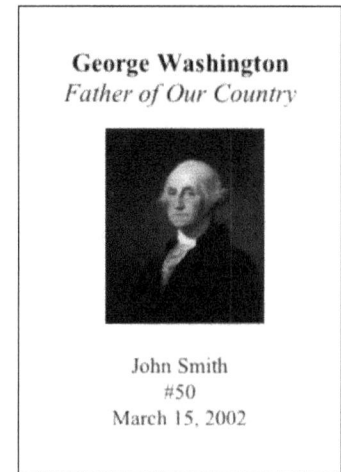

George Washington
Father of Our Country

John Smith
#50
March 15, 2002

7. Assemble the pages in this order:

   Title page

   Body of report

   Bibliography

   Maps, charts, or pictures not included in the body of the paper

   Outline (both the edited and the corrected one)

   Edited (by teacher) rough draft

   Grading rubric page

8. Attach all pages in a binder with a clear plastic front. Use a binder with three brads to hold the paper. **Do not use a slide lock.**

Name_____ Date ___/___/____ Class #____

Attach this page to the back of your final copy.

Grading rubric for FINAL COPY about a PERSON from history

Name, date, class number, guidelines page attached	**10**
Introduction with thesis statement	**10**
Early life of person (topic sentence) birth: place, date; family: father, mother, siblings; education: schools attended, course of study or trade; physical description	**20**
Historical background (topic sentence) political; cultural; religious beliefs; economic; controversies; position regarding major issues of the time	**20**
Accomplishments (topic sentence) (The main body of your paper, two to three paragraphs) In chronological order, give details of person's life from young adulthood until later life.	**40**
Later life (topic sentence) family life; spouse, children; events not listed under accomplishments; death: cause, year and age, last words (if known)	**20**
Application of person's life and accomplishments (topic sentence) (How is the world different today because he or she lived?)	**20**
Concluding paragraph (topic sentence) General info, wrap up paper	**10**
Footnotes: At least three direct quotes by or about your person in proper footnote form	**10**
Style Grammar, usage, spelling, punctuation, capitalization Sentence construction is varied and interesting	**20**
Presentation Typed, double spaced, bound in a clear, flat report folder with brads Bibliography and outline Title page and picture of person Other illustrations **Edited rough draft attached**	**20**
TOTAL	**200**

WHY I WROTE THIS BOOK

Twenty years ago, I, a math teacher, taught composition for the first time. I found myself faced with the task of teaching three classes of sixth-graders at an expensive private school how to write a research paper for their science fair projects. What would I do? First, I prayed for wisdom.

Next, I went to each of the elementary teachers to learn how they taught writing and found, to my dismay, that everyone did it a different way. So I decided to go straight to the top and ask the head of the high school English department how she did it. I wanted to prepare my students for high school and have them learn the right way to write.

Arriean Schemer was patient with me and answered all of my questions. She had a big banner on her classroom wall that said

How do we eat the elephant? One bite at a time.

That has turned into my life's maxim, from teaching how to complete a big, overwhelming task, to making myself do the same thing. One step at a time does it.

I learned a lot of things the hard way, like filling out bibliography cards *before* you return the books to the library. I assembled information from many sources into a research paper booklet that

I revised and edited every year, eventually replacing all the information with my own instructions, examples, and advice.

What you hold in your hands is over 20 years' worth of experience in reading and editing probably thousands of essays and research papers. After six years at the private school, I started my own middle school for homeschool children. They come to my class one day a week and are taught by their moms or dads the other four days. I put together the curriculum, and a major part of what we do every year is to write a research paper.

My first students have graduated from college, married, and had children. I hear over and over how they took their research paper booklets with them to high school and college and were the ones to help everyone else learn to write a paper. They tell me how their English teachers asked them, "Where did you learn to write like this?" I can't describe the joy and satisfaction it gives me to know I have helped them stand out above the rest and learn to communicate effectively.

I decided to publish the book not only for my own students and their families, but also for everyone else. Whether you are using it for an elementary report or a doctoral thesis, I hope you will find it useful and that it will be a blessing to you as you eat that elephant of a paper.

Every day I start out asking God to give me wisdom, and that includes the writing of this booklet. It is my pleasure to share some of that wisdom with you.

About the Author

Ceil Baker Humphreys has been involved in education her entire life. Teaching runs in the family, as her mother and sister Posy were also educators. She lives in Orlando, Florida, with Wesley, her husband of 40 years. Ceil is the proud mother of two sons, Robert and Michael, and the grandmother of Jheison, Kevin, Leah, Cade, and Isabella—and another, Christina, on the way.

Mrs. Humphreys has taught public, private, and home school. Since 1997, she has been the owner/teacher at Humphreys Junior High, a one-day-a-week academic program for homeschooled students in grades five through eight.

"When teachers die and go to heaven, they get to do what I do," she tells friends. "Life is good, and God is good. I feel like He has blessed me so much."

In her spare time she enjoys reading and doing any kind of needlework, including embroidery, crochet, and knitting. In her fantasy life, she owns a sheep farm and spins her own wool. But back to reality.

Designing counted cross stitch kits for her sister's company, the Posy Collection, earns Ceil mad money and has also helped her learn a lot about history from the historic sites that sell the designs. Her first design was of Monticello, the home of Thomas Jefferson, one of her heroes, and Mount Vernon, home of her superhero, George Washington, carries more of her designs than any other site. The kits can be seen at **posycollection.com**.

But her favorite thing of all is being with her loved ones, including her relatives, church family, and friends.

For more information about Pine Ridge Home Educators, where Humphreys Junior High is located, visit **prhe.net**.